Speaking Frames: How to Teach Talk for Writing: Ages 10–14

Now revised and expanded, *Speaking Frames: How to Teach Talk for Writing: Ages 10–14* brings together material from Sue Palmer's popular Speaking Frames books with additional material covering the primary/secondary transition. Providing an innovative and effective answer to the problem of teaching speaking and listening, this book offers a range of speaking frames for children to 'fill in' orally, developing their language patterns and creativity, and boosting their confidence in the use of literate language. Fully updated, this book offers:

- material for individual paired and group presentations and talk for writing;
- links to cross-curricular 'skeletons';
- transition material and guidance on 'bridging the gap' between primary and secondary schools;
- support notes for teachers and assessment guidance;
- advice on flexible progression and working to a child's ability;
- suggestions for developing individual pupils' spoken language skills.

With a wealth of photocopiable sheets and creative ideas for speaking and listening, *Speaking Frames: How to Teach Talk for Writing: Ages 10–14* is essential reading for all practising, trainee and recently qualified teachers who wish to develop effective speaking and listening in their classroom.

Sue Palmer is a writer, broadcaster and education consultant. Specialising in the teaching of literacy, she has authored over 150 books and has contributed to numerous television programmes and software packages. She is the author of *How to Teach Writing Across the Curriculum: Ages 6–8* and *How to Teach Writing Across the Curriculum: Ages 8–14*, also published by Routledge.

D0899756

Also available:

Speaking Frames: How to Teach Talk for Writing: Ages 8–10
Sue Palmer
(ISBN: 978-0-415-57982-7)

Speaking Frames: How to Teach Talk for Writing: Ages 10–14

Sue Palmer

Routledge
Taylor & Francis Group

LONDON AND NEW YORK

This first edition published 2011
by Routledge
2 Park Square, Milton Park, Abingdon, Oxon, OX14 4RN

Simultaneously published in the USA and Canada
by Routledge
270 Madison Avenue, New York, NY 10016

Routledge is an imprint of the Taylor & Francis Group, an informa business

© 2011 Sue Palmer

Typeset in Helvetica by FiSH Books. Enfield
Printed and bound in Great Britain by the MPG Books Group

British Library Cataloguing in Publication Data
A catalogue record for this book is available from the British Library

Library of Congress Cataloging-in-Publication Data
Palmer, Sue, 1948–
    Speaking frames : how to teach talk for writing, ages 10–14 / by Sue Palmer.
        p. cm.
    1. English language—Composition and exercises—Study and teaching (Secondary) 2. English language—Composition and exercises—Study and teaching (Elementary) 3. English language—Spoken English. I. Title.
    LB1631.P23 2011
    428.0071—dc22

                                                                            2010005032

ISBN13: 978-0-415-57987-2 (pbk)
ISBN13: 978-0-203-84636-0 (ebk)

Contents

Introducing speaking frames

Speaking frames are frameworks for directed speaking and listening activities. They are specifically designed to help students move from the patterns of spoken language to the more complex patterns of written language and 'literate talk'. In this way, it is hoped they will help develop students' control over language in both speaking and writing.

Spoken and written language patterns

It is now well established that written language is very different from the spoken variety. Speech is generally interactive – we bat words and phrases back and forth – and produced within a shared context, so it's fragmented, disorganised and a great deal of meaning goes by on the nod. In fact, you can get by in speech without ever forming a conventional sentence, or at least only very simple ones. To make links between ideas, speakers tend to use very simple connectives, like the ubiquitous *and* or, to denote sequence, *and then.* This kind of language is described by linguists as 'spontaneous speech'.

On the other hand, written language is produced for an unknown, unseen audience, who may have no background knowledge at all about the subject. It must therefore be explicit and carefully crafted. It requires more extensive vocabulary than speech and organisation into sentences for clarity. The sentences become increasingly complex as the writer expresses increasingly complex ideas, using a widening range of connectives to show how these ideas relate to each other.

The interface between speech and writing

The more 'literate' someone is, the more these written language patterns also begin to inform their speech. Exposure to literate language through reading, and the opportunity to develop control of it oneself, through writing, leads to increasingly literate spoken language. It seems to be a cyclical process: speech informs writing, which then informs speech, which informs writing, and so on. In general, the more accomplished the writer, the better equipped he or she is to 'talk like a book'.

Until the late nineteenth century, this interface between speech and writing was universally acknowledged. From the time of the ancient Greeks, **rhetoric** (reading aloud, speaking persuasively) was considered as essential a part of education as reading and writing – perhaps even more so. Exercises in rhetoric were intended to develop not only pupils' powers of oratory, but also their ear for language – the explicit, complex patterns of language in which educated people converse and write. As Ben Jonson put it in 1640:

For a man to write well, there are required three necessaries: to read the best authors, to hear the best speakers, and much exercise of his own style.

However, the introduction of universal state education automatically meant large classes in which speech for the many was not deemed possible (or desirable), and the literacy curriculum was restricted to reading and writing. Throughout the twentieth century, educators have concentrated their attention on literacy, at the expense of oracy. Speaking frames provide a twenty-first century approach to the forgotten 'fourth R'.

The 'two horses' model

Speaking frames were initially developed as an aid to writing. Teaching students to write without first giving opportunities to speak is, fairly obviously, 'putting the cart before the horse'. However, opportunities for talk before writing do not necessarily develop literate language patterns. Ideally, there should be two 'oracy horses' drawing the 'writing cart'.

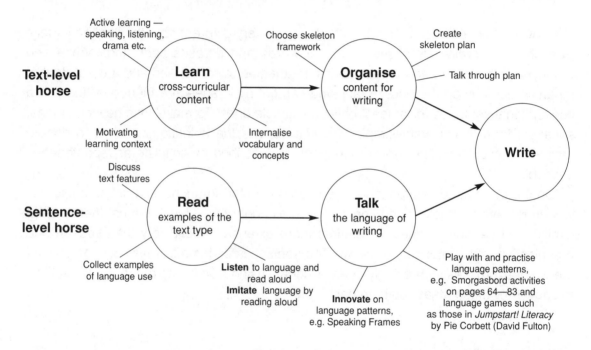

Figure 1 Two horses before the cart model

The first 'horse' operates at text level – 'talk for learning'. These spoken language activities are vital for helping students to:

- engage with the subject under discussion;
- familiarise themselves with key vocabulary;
- get to grips with underlying concepts;
- organise their ideas appropriately before they write.

The talk will generally be interactive, context-dependent and conducted in the language of spontaneous speech. There are many suggestions for providing 'talk for learning' in *How to Teach Writing Across the Curriculum: Ages 8–14* (Routledge, 2011).

The second is a sentence level horse – 'talk for writing'. This is the opportunity for students to develop knowledge about and familiarity with the sorts of language appropriate to the writing task. Speaking frames were developed as a means of focusing on elements of literate language which express ideas clearly and coherently for an unknown audience.

Listen – Imitate – Innovate – Invent

There is a well established developmental model for the way children acquire speech: first they **listen** to adult speakers and **imitate** elements of their speech; then they begin to **innovate** on these language patterns; finally they use all this language data to **invent** their own expressions. However, in terms of acquiring written language patterns – which are, indeed, much more demanding in terms of form and complexity – we make little provision for the first three stages. All too often, we ask children to go straight to invention.

For students with a strong background of literacy this may not be a problem. If they come from families where 'literate talk' is the norm, they may well absorb and reproduce many of its features as naturally as we all acquire spontaneous speech patterns. There is another group of children who are likely to absorb written language patterns without effort, whatever their social background. These are the ones who learn to read easily, and who then become committed readers, tackling a wide range of reading matter. They'll pick up written language patterns through frequent exposure to the printed page. However, in a multimedia world, where young people can access all the entertainment and information they want via visual displays on a screen, fewer and fewer of them are reading widely in their leisure time. For the majority of students, unless we provide structured help, learning to write will be inhibited by a lack of appropriate vocabulary, language constructions and cohesive devices.

Integrating 'Listen – Imitate – Innovate – Invent' into teaching

Most English teachers now spend time, before students write, familiarising them with key aspects of the particular text type – building up a 'writer's toolkit' of organisational and linguistic features. Many of these language patterns are unfamiliar to students – opportunities to listen, imitate and innovate can develop familiarity and help students internalise the linguistic features so that they are available both for writing and for literate talk.

- **Listen**: students need opportunities to *hear* literate language as often as possible, to become familiar with the rhythms and patterns of sentences, and of specific phrases and constructions particularly useful for a text type.
- **Imitate**: they also need the chance to produce literate language patterns from their own mouths – to know how more sophisticated vocabulary and phraseology *feels*, and to respond physically to the ebb and flow of well-constructed sentences.
- **Innovate**: then they need opportunities to innovate on those patterns, expressing their own ideas and understanding through the medium of literate talk.

One way of ensuring students **listen** to and **imitate** written language patterns is through reading aloud to them and ensuring they have plenty of opportunities to read aloud themselves (paired reading with a partner – one paragraph each – is a good way of ensuring the latter). However, it is difficult to target specific language patterns in this way, and reading aloud does not provide an opportunity to **innovate**.

Figure 2 The patterns of written language

How speaking frames work

Speaking frames replicate the listen – imitate – innovate model for specific types of language as part of students' learning across the curriculum. In pairs, groups or as individuals, they work on a specific task and fit their answers into a given frame for oral presentation to the class. The class therefore **listens** to a number of presentations based on the frame:

- first by the teacher, as he or she demonstrates the process;
- next by more able students, selected by the teacher as likely to provide good and fluent models;
- then by their remaining peers.

And every student has an opportunity to **imitate** and **innovate** on the same language patterns as they make their own presentation.

Nine specific speaking frames are provided, as a starting point for teachers and students. There is also a 'smorgasbord' of useful sentence starts relating to the sorts of talking and writing students undertake across the curriculum. Teachers can use these as they are (for instance, using the teaching suggestions given with each photocopiable page) and/or take from them to make further speaking frames based on the cross-curricular work or literacy objectives being pursued by the class.

The importance of literate talk

Although speaking frames were originally devised to help students get to grips with written language, their potential for the development of oral language skills is perhaps even more important. The frames facilitate the virtuous circle described above of 'speech informs writing . . . informs speech . . . informs writing . . . informs speech . . .', and thus should help develop students' powers of literate speech as much they develop written work.

Many students find speaking in front of an audience difficult, often because they do not have access to patterns of literate talk. Trapped in spontaneous spoken language patterns, their vocabulary is limited and speech is fragmented, incoherent and lacking in organisation. Speaking frames provide support in translating their ideas into coherent sentences, and preparing their presentation gives time to consider vocabulary, develop explicitness and experiment with more formal connectives than they would usually use. Practice makes perfect, and the opportunities provided here to practise presentation skills should also develop students' confidence, social skills and self-esteem.

In the modern world, there's another hugely important reason for developing powers of literate talk. As the use of voice-activated software proliferates in the workplace, 'writers' of the future may seldom actually *write* very much at all. They'll be expected to compose and dictate texts directly into machines. This requires excellent command of spoken language – so 'talk for writing' may in the long run be more important than writing itself.

The 'two horses' model for teaching was developed with this probability in mind. It therefore prepares students to learn, organise and record their understanding at text level, then 'talk it into print' at sentence level – for further information on this process see Appendix on pages 84–90 and *How to Teach Writing Across the Curriculum: Ages 8–14* (Routledge, 2011). While the physical act of writing is essential as children acquire literacy skills, in their adult lives the successful production of text is likely to depend far more on their capacity for literate talk. If young people don't acquire this linguistic skill, their capacity to communicate in print may be limited to the speech-like patterns of 'emailese'.

A note on assessment

The speaking frames provided are for three types of presentation: students working in pairs, as individuals and in groups of around six. Each type of presentation requires preliminary teaching, which can be covered using the three sample frames.

Speaking and listening are notoriously difficult to assess, and this is particularly the case with 'talk for writing', where many social, intellectual and linguistic sub-skills are brought together in reaching the final presentation. This book breaks the student's performance into four elements, covered in two teaching sections:

- Section 1: Introducing the activity;
  - **preparation** for the presentation
  - the **content** of the presentation.
- Section 2: Staging the presentation;
  - specific **language** use in the presentation (moving towards literate language)
  - **presentation** skills.

Because so many skills are involved, it is difficult to be precise about teaching objectives. Teachers will obviously concentrate on objectives as appropriate to students' ability and experience.

However, too much emphasis on specific objectives here could lead to very reductionist teaching. The activities cover many aspects of the literacy curriculum as well as cross-curricular thinking skills, social skills and the development of self-confidence as a speaker. The true learning objective is the orchestration of all these skills in pursuit of a clearly defined outcome: the presentation itself. While the teacher may choose to emphasise a particular aspect of any of the four elements listed above, it should always be seen within the context of the whole activity.

Simple assessment sheets are provided for each of the types of presentation, to help teachers focus on the performance of specific students, pairs or groups. Another means of assessment is to video or audiotape students' presentations and ask them to assess their own performance using the *Giving the Talk* sheet as a checklist.

Paired presentations

Paired work is the easiest type of speaking frame presentation. Students who have previously used a 'talking partners' technique should adjust to using frames quickly; for those who have not used the technique, the frames are an ideal introduction.

Preparatory materials

Stage 1: Tell the Aliens

In the three *Tell the Aliens* activities, pairs of students develop and present a series of short talks involving clear description and explanation. The frames are couched in more formal 'literate language' than students generally use, and the need for complete clarity (so the aliens will understand) encourages them to use more explicit language. Students who are used to the restricted, implicit language of speech often feel that this level of description is 'stating the obvious', but such explicitness is essential for the understanding and communication of ideas in many areas of the curriculum:

- **Task 1: *How it works*** involves analysing and describing the characteristics of a familiar object, and explaining how it works.
- **Task 2: *What it's like*** involves describing a familiar item of clothing with as great a degree of explicitness as possible.
- **Task 3**: ***How to play*** involves analysing what is involved in playing a particular team game, and explaining the rules.

Stage 2: Critical evaluation

In these activities, pairs of students develop and present a series of short critical talks on fiction, poetry and non-fiction texts. The frames are couched in more formal 'literate language' than students generally use, and encourage the pairs to explain and justify their reactions to the texts.

- **Task 1: *Fiction*** involves summarising the plot of a fiction book, and commenting critically on plot, style and characterisation, giving evidence from the text to back up their views.
- **Task 2: *Poem*** involves summarising the main theme or message of the poem, and commenting critically on theme/message, style and imagery or word play, giving evidence for the text to back up their views.
- **Task 3**: ***Non-fiction*** involves selecting a non-fiction book for a specific research task, scanning it to determine its usefulness, using the index to identify parts which would be useful, reading for information and commenting critically on the usefulness of the book, providing examples from the text to support their views.

The activities give students the chance to hear appropriate 'literate language' patterns issuing from their own mouths, prior (it is to be hoped) to using them in written work, and to develop their control of technical terminology. They specifically cover these aspects of literate talk:

- speaking in complete sentences, using a variety of complex sentence constructions;
- varying sentence construction (including a variety of sentence openings – adverbials, subordinate clauses);
- the standard English '... and I' (as opposed to 'Me and ...');
- the language of exemplification (*For instance, For example* – more on page 74);
- formal language structures, including the use of the passive voice (e.g. *It is used for... which is worn on... the game is played...*);
- techniques for defining technical terminology (e.g. *which is a... that is...*);
- the language of opinion (*In our opinion... We think...* etc) and justification through reference to the text (*For instance, at one point... A typical example can be found on page...* etc.).
- appropriate language for commenting on the effects of text (e.g. *effective, ineffective, successful, unsuccessful*).

GETTING READY
STAGE 1: TELL THE ALIENS

1. Study the frame and decide what you are going to talk about. Make sure you know all the facts about it – or how you can find them out.

2. Read each section of the frame, and discuss how to finish it, so that it will be perfectly clear to an alien who has never seen such a thing. Jot down key words to remind you.

3. Practise your presentation together, taking turns to say one section each. Listen to each other and suggest improvements, e.g.

   – more precise language
   – extra detail
   – clearer explanation.

4. When you are happy that your talk is perfect, practise till you can do it easily.

GETTING READY
STAGE 2: CRITICAL EVALUATION

1. Study the frame and decide which text you are going to talk about. Make sure you, have a copy of the text, know it well and share an opinion about it.

2. Read each section of the frame, and discuss how to finish it. Jot down key words to remind you and either copy out examples or mark them clearly in your copy of the text.

3. Practise your presentation together, taking turns to say one section each. Listen to each other and suggest improvements, e.g.

    – better phrasing of ideas
    – clearer speaking/reading of examples
    – more fluent use of the frame.

4. When you are happy that your talk is perfect, practise till you can do it easily.

Introducing paired presentations

- Display an enlarged copy of the appropriate 'Getting Ready' notes and the relevant speaking frame.
- Read the frame with students. Explain the aim:
  - in *Tell the Aliens*, to develop explicit language – clear, precise description, which is needed in many cross-curricular tasks. If you assume the aliens know absolutely nothing, you have to think very hard about how to describe familiar objects and processes
  - in *Critical Evaluation,* to develop critical reading/appreciation of a text and the vocabulary/language structures used to explore and express these ideas.
- If this sort of activity is new to your students, in Stage 1 it may help to go through the 'Getting Ready' notes, and demonstrate each stage yourself, working with a partner. You could model the sorts of behaviour and outcomes you are looking for, as in the 'points to watch for' boxes below.
- Go through the 'Getting Ready' notes, and demonstrate each stage, working with a partner yourself. Model the sorts of behaviour and outcome you are looking for, as in the 'points to watch for' boxes below.
- Give out small copies of the frame for students to work with.

Give the pairs an appropriate amount of time to decide exactly what they are going to say, and to rehearse it (if they need to check out facts, preparation will take longer). Watch how the pairs interact, and make sure they know you're watching. Tell them you won't necessarily intervene if things are not going well: they have to learn to work cooperatively, and can't always rely on you to sort out problems. You could use the assessment sheet on page 22 to focus on the work of some pairs.

Points to watch for during preparation

Collaboration	Are they sharing tasks and ideas? Is one partner dominating? Have they found or made a visual aid? In criticising a text, do they share opinions or have to compromise?
Reflecting on content	Are they taking time talking through each section?
Refining ideas	Do their ideas develop, change, improve through discussion?
Note-making	Do notes cover keywords for the presentation? Are both partners involved in making notes?
Practice	Do they practise? Do they use practice to improve content and presentation? Do they give useful feedback to each other?

Points to watch for in content

Choice of topic	Is it a mutual choice? Is it suitable/interesting?
Accuracy/ research	Are their statements/descriptions factually accurate or their opinion valid? If necessary, are they able to find out information/evidence?
Effectiveness	Are they providing the bare minimum response or looking for more engaging detail and means of expression?
Keywords	Are they choosing good keywords – precise nouns, suitable adjectives, good choice of verbs?

Don't interrupt students who are going well. Where you decide intervention is necessary, use questioning strategies to help them on course, e.g.:

- *If you don't agree, how can you find a solution?*
- *Where could you go to find a good word?*

Give positive feedback about the discussions at the end of the session, e.g.:

- *I liked the way Andrew and Asif negotiated solutions.*
- *I thought Maria and Shara were enterprising the way they used the thesaurus.*

Then move straight into presentation – see next page.

GIVING THE TALK

1. Ensure you know who is going to say each section, so you move fluently from one to the other.

2. When you are presenting, try to appear confident and in control:

- Look at the audience.
- Speak slowly, loudly and clearly enough for everyone to hear every word.
- Stand still, with good posture, and don't fidget.
- If you look confident, you'll start to feel confident.

3. If anything goes wrong, try to get back on course without any fuss. Support your partner, and let your partner support you.

Staging paired presentations

Display an enlarged copy of the *Giving the Talk* notes opposite, and talk through them with students, drawing attention to the key points in the box. Choose a few pairs of students who are ready and ask them to present their talks while the class listens.

Points to watch for in language

Sentence structure	Do they use the frame to speak in sentences? Does their expression indicate awareness of grammatical boundaries? Are any extra sentences framed correctly?
Explicitness	Is the description clear and explicit? Have they added necessary detail?
Vocabulary	Is vocabulary varied or repetitive? Have they used precise nouns, suitable adjectives and verbs?
Standard English	Have they used the vocabulary and grammar of standard English?

Points to watch for in presentation

Turn-taking/ collaboration	Is their turn-talking organised or chaotic? Do they work together or as two individuals? If necessary, do they help each other out?
Pace	Is delivery of each speaker too fast or too slow?
Voice	Is each speaker audible? Are voices expressive or monotonous?
Audience engagement	Do they address the audience or each other? Do they use any visual aids effectively?
Body language	Do they stand confidently or self-consciously? Do they use gesture to enhance speech? Do they wriggle or fuss with their notes?
Dealing with problems	Are they easily distracted? If anything goes wrong do they deal with it satisfactorily?

Give brief feedback to the pair on key points of their performance. Give specific praise wherever possible, e.g.:

- *I really liked the way you used' object' or 'item' rather than 'thing'.*
- *You adapted the speaking frame to your needs really well.*
- *I was impressed by the way you took turns, with each person's speech flowing on from the other's.*

Where feedback is negative, give it from the point of view of the audience, e.g.:

- *Sometimes it was difficult to hear because you were speaking very quickly.*

- *You have such a quiet voice we couldn't hear everything you said.*
- *I was distracted by the way you were fiddling with your paper.*

Invite the rest of the class to comment on aspects of the performance (perhaps basing it on the *Giving the Talk* notes), ensuring the criticism is constructive. As students become more experienced at giving paired presentations, feedback can become more detailed and specific.

If each presentation and feedback takes about five to eight minutes, you should be able to hear about six pairs at a time while still maintaining the interest of the class. Some pairs may also need more time to prepare. Provide further time as necessary, then give opportunities for all the pairs to present their talks, about six or so at a time.

■ Tell the aliens

HOW IT WORKS

_____ and I are going to explain how a
_____ works .

A _____ is a type of _____
which is used for _____ .

It usually consists of _____ (detailed description) _____
_____
_____ .

When you use a _____ , you _____
(detailed description)
_____
_____ .

The sort of person who would use a _____
is a _____ or _____ .

For instance, _____
_____ .

'**Lewis** and I are going to explain how a **screwdriver** works.

A **screwdriver** is a type of **tool** which is used for **fixing screws into place to hold things together and also for taking the screws out.**

It usually consists of **a long thin metal rod with a plastic handle at one end. At the other end the metal rod narrows into the correct shape to fit in the hole in the screw. Sometimes the hole is like a ridge and the screwdriver ends in a thin strip that fits the ridge. On a Philips-head screw, it is more like a lot of little holes, so the screwdriver ends in a lot of little points to fit in the holes.**

When you use a **screwdriver**, you **put the metal end into the hole in the screw. Holding onto the handle, you turn the screwdriver round and round, and this turns the screw round. This either forces the screw into place, or loosens it out of the place it's in.**

The sort of person who would use a **screwdriver** is a **carpenter, builder, maintenance worker** or **engineer.**

For instance, **a carpenter would use it when fixing two pieces of wood together with screws.**'

Talk about:

- The importance of (a) choosing something simple (b) understanding **exactly** how it works before trying to explain it.
- Choosing an item to talk about, e.g.:

bottle opener	watch strap	key and lock
zip	light switch	clasp on a necklace or bracelet
paperclip	three pin plug	pencil sharpener
elastic band	door catch	umbrella
scissors	Sellotape dispenser	compass
stapler	mousetrap	eggtimer

  You could give a list for students to choose from. Don't worry if several students choose the same item – the comparisons will be interesting.
- Words that might fit into the first sentence, e.g. *tool, machine, utensil, mechanism*.
- What's important in describing such items (e.g. size, shape, design, functionality) and what's not particularly important (e.g. colour, pattern).
- Thinking about how things work, and how to explain them.
- Being very explicit – not worrying about 'stating the obvious'. Remember: Aliens know nothing.
- The changes necessary if the item is plural, e.g. scissors, needle and thread. Use postit notes to show the changes:

  _____ are a type of _____ . They usually consist of _____, etc.

- Changing *a* to *an* if the item begins with a vowel, e.g. elastic band, umbrella.
- Using 'grown up' language constructions and vocabulary, such as *container*.
- Building up the description as you plan your talk.

■ Tell the aliens

WHAT IT'S LIKE
(an item of clothing)

_____ and I are going to describe a _____ .

A _____ is an item of clothing which is worn on _____ .

It usually consists of _____ (detailed description)
_____ .

_____ are usually made of _____
_____ .

They may have _____ .

The sort of person who would wear a _____ is _____ . For example _____ .

'**Diamond** and I are going to describe a **top**.

A **top** is an item of clothing which is worn on **the upper part of the body.**

It usually consists of **a main part, which covers the body from the neck to the waist area, a collar for the head to go through, and armholes for the arms to go through. Many tops also have two sleeves, which may be long or short. These come out of the armholes and cover the arms. Tops without sleeves are called sleeveless tops.**

Tops are usually made of **cotton or a similar lightweight fabric, and may be plain or patterned. Some tops – such as tee-shirts – are tight, while others – like smock-tops – may be baggy.**

They may have **buttons, press studs or a zip to hold them together – these could be either on the front or the back of the top.**

The sort of person who would wear a top is **a woman or girl.** For example, **most teenagers wear tops with either jeans or a skirt.**'

Talk about:

● Choosing an item of clothing. Alert them to the possibilities, e.g.:

outdoor wear	school uniform	swimwear
nightwear	footwear	headgear

specialist clothing for soldiers, firefighters, bakers, etc..

Suggest they get or make visual aids to help with their talk.
● The sorts of detail to put into their description, e.g. shape, size, texture, weight or dimensions.
● Thinking of all the possible variations and describing them too.
● Specific 'scientific' vocabulary, e.g. *fabric, upper/lower body*.
● Changes necessary if the item is plural, e.g. trousers, tights, leggings. Use sticky notes to show the changes:

They usually consist of . . .

● Changing *a* to *an* if the item begins with a vowel, e.g. apron.
● Building up the description as you plan your talk.
● Ways in which the frame allows you to 'hedge your bets', e.g. *usually, they may have . . .* Many written descriptions require this tentative language, as there are usually wide variations.

■ Tell the aliens

HOW TO PLAY

_____ and I are going to explain how to play _____, which involves two teams. We shall call them Team A and Team B. _____ .

The game is played _____ (where) _____ –
that is a _____ (description) _____ .

In order to play you need _____ ,
which is/are _____ .

To start the game, _____ .

Continue, explaining a step each, choosing suitable connectives, e.g.

Then _____ .

While _____ .

If_____ , _____ .

The aim of the game is _____ .

'**Imran** and I are going to explain how to play **cricket,** which involves two teams. We shall call them Team A and Team B. **There are eleven players in each team.**

The game is played **on a cricket pitch – that is a large field covered in short grass with a section in the middle called the wicket. The wicket is a strip of very flat grass 22 yards long, and at each end there are three sticks, known as stumps. The sticks stand upright and across the top there are some little pieces of wood called bails.**

In order to play you need **the two sets of stumps, a small hard ball, and at least two cricket bats which are like flat wooden clubs. You use these to hit the ball. You should also have a set of playing clothes (shirt, trousers and cricket shoes with small studs in the bottom) and some protective clothing for batsmen and wicket keeper. The most important protective gear is the pads, which are padded covers for the legs, and the box, which you wear under your trousers to protect your private parts.**

To start the game, **Team A comes out on to the pitch – they will be bowling and fielding (which means collecting the ball when a batsman has hit it). Team B send out two batsmen, and one stands at each wicket.** Then **a bowler from Team A bowls the ball (an overarm throw) at the first batsman, trying to hit the wicket behind him. If he hits the wicket the batsman is out, and another batsman comes on instead of him. Other ways a batsman might be out include using his leg instead of his bat to defend his wicket (Leg Before Wicket) or being caught (that is, he hits the ball and before it bounces one of the fielders catches it).**

On the other hand, if the batsman is able to hit the ball with the bat, and it goes far enough away for him to run right down the wicket and swap ends with his friend, that is called a run. Batsmen sometimes get two or three runs. If they hit the ball beyond the edge of the field (the boundary) without it touching the ground, they get six free runs, and if it touches the ground but still goes over the boundary, they get four free runs. When **all the batsmen on Team B are out, they swap over and Team A bats.**

The aim of the game is **for one team to score more runs than the other.**'

Talk about:

- Choosing a game. It's important to choose a game you know well, e.g.:

football	rounders	hockey	basketball
netball	relay race	rugby	five-a-side

    Some students may choose card or board games.
- Suggest they make or find visual aids to help with their talk, e.g. a plan of a soccer pitch and some pictures of the game in progress would be very helpful.
- The necessity of defining technical terminology. They need to become aware of the sorts of vocabulary that a non-enthusiast wouldn't know.
- Summarising complex rules – explanations shouldn't drag on and on (practice is really important here).

■ Critical evaluation

FICTION

_____ and I have been discussing _____
by _____ . This book, which was first
published in _____ is about _____ .

On the whole, we (dis)liked the plot because
_____ . For instance, at one point,
_____ .

The book is narrated by _____ . This has
the effect of _____ !

In terms of style, we (dis)liked the way the author
_____ .
A typical example of this can be found on page
_____, where _____ .

We think the characterisation is (in)effective. For
instance _____ .

Our overall verdict on the book is _____ .

'**Liam** and I have been discussing *Cue for Treason* by **Geoffrey Trease.** This book, which was first published in **1940**, is about **a boy called Peter Brownrigg in Elizabethan times, who has to go on the run from the law and ends up joining a group of travelling players and meeting William Shakespeare. Peter and his friend Kit accidentally discover a plot to murder Queen Elizabeth, and have many different adventures as they try to foil the plotters and save the queen.**

On the whole, we liked the plot because **it was exciting. No sooner was one nail-biting episode over than another began!** For instance, at one point, **Peter escapes from a snobby nobleman who is chasing him by hiding in a 'coffin' in the theatre. The actors find him and save him from Sir Philip, but in no time at all he's in danger again from an unknown 'watcher' who attacks him during the night.**

The book is narrated by **Peter himself, so it is a first person narrative.** This has the effect of **making everything more immediate and tense, because you go through the adventure with Peter, and know all his feelings. It also means you are sometimes misled, just as Peter is – for instance, one of the characters is definitely not what he seems to be at first!**

In terms of style, we liked the way the author **uses the first person narrative to make you feel as though you are there.** A typical example of this can be found on page **152**, where **he's exploring a dark tower:** *I felt my way down stair by stair, down into the gloom of the store cellar. One, two, three, four ... at each step I paused and listened. I wished I had a candle.* Then some people come in behind him: *I stood where I was, my pistol cocked. Were they coming all the way down? No, apparently.* **He uses questions and short sentences to make it sound like Peter's thoughts and to keep up the suspense.**

We think the characterisation is effective. For instance, **Shakespeare comes over as a very understanding person, which he must have been in order to write his plays. Queen Elizabeth appears at the very end, and Peter doesn't dare look at her much, but when he kisses her hand it's** *gnarled – The brown fingers were knobbly with too many rings.* **From this you can guess she is old and very ornately dressed. When she speaks she has** *a brisk voice* **and she swears and** *barks* **her orders.**

Our overall verdict on the book is **that it is a brilliant adventure story that also teaches you about life in Elizabethan England and inspires interest in Shakespeare and his plays.'**

Talk about:

- Choosing a book to evaluate: it must be one both partners know very well.
- Adjusting the frame according to whether you like or dislike the book (cross out prefixes, etc. as necessary). Ensure students recognise that they must be able to justify all opinions, producing evidence from the text.
- Adjusting the wording of the frame if necessary to fit their own critique.
- Finding different points to make about plot, narration, style and characterisation (it may be that they like some aspects of the book but not others).
- Ensuring that they have any examples of text to hand, either by copying them out or by marking the passages in the book.

■ Critical evaluation

POEM

_____ and I have been discussing _____ by
_____ . This is a classic/modern poem about
_____ .

> The main theme/message of the poem is
> _____ . We found this (un)interesting
> because _____ .

The style of the poem is illustrated in this extract:

_____ .

We think this is (in)effective because _____

_____ .

> The poet uses imagery/word play such as
> _____ . In our opinion, this is
> (un)successful because _____ .

We think the best/worst line in the poem is
_____ . We (dis)like them because

_____ .

> On the whole, this poem makes us feel _____
> because _____ .

'**Chris** and I have been discussing '**The Charge of the Light Brigade'** by **Alfred, Lord Tennyson.** This is a classic poem about **a brigade of soldiers in the Crimean War, who were given the wrong orders. They were told to charge directly at the enemy's guns. When they obeyed the order, most of the soldiers died.** Tennyson **was Poet Laureate at the time and he wrote this poem to commemorate them.**

The poem's main message is **that the Charge of the Light Brigade was glorious because the soldiers put duty before their own lives.** We found this interesting because **nowadays the excuse that 'I was only following orders' is not considered a very good one, and the newspapers tell us that suicide bombers are evil.**

The style of the poem is illustrated in this extract:

> *"Forward, the Light Brigade!" / Was there a man dismayed? / Not though the soldier knew / Someone had blundered. / Theirs not to make reply, / Theirs not to reason why, / Theirs but to do and die: / Into the Valley of Death / Rode the six hundred.*

We think this is effective because **the rhyme and repetition carry you along like the soldiers' horses. The repetition of** *Theirs* **hammers home the importance of duty. The last two lines have a slower rhythm that makes them seem more solemn.**

The poet uses imagery such as *jaws of Death, mouth of Hell.* In our opinion, this is successful **because the images conjured up are simple but terrifying.**

We think the best lines in the poem are *Stormed at with shot and shell, / While horse and hero fell, / They that had fought so well / Came through the jaws of Death, / Back from the mouth of Hell, / All that was left of them, / Left of six hundred.* We like them because **they repeat lots of lines we've heard before, but this time they're coming back and we realise most of the soldiers are dead. Tennyson doesn't say how many were left, but we've found out it was about 200 – so one out of three died.**

On the whole, the poem makes us feel **sad but proud** because **although it was a mistake, Tennyson makes you see the glory of what they did. It also makes you understand how other nations might feel differently from us about their suicide bombers.**

Talk about:

- Choosing a poem: generally it is easier to explain and justify why you like a poem than why you dislike it.
- Adjusting the frame and wording as necessary to fit their own critique.
- What is meant by the 'theme or message' of the poem.
- Elements of style (e.g. rhyme, rhythm, repetition, onomatopoeia, alliteration, etc. and choosing a section which illustrates it.
- Deciding on whether your poem uses imagery (simile, metaphor, personification) or word play (puns, riddles, homophones).
- Choosing a favourite (or most hated) line or lines and justifying your choice.
- How to deal with extracts and examples. Will you copy them out and read them, or learn them by heart.

■ *Critical evaluation*

NON-FICTION

_____ and I want to find out about _____ so we chose this book, called _____ . It was written by _____ in _____ .

> When we scanned the contents page, headings and pictures, we thought it would/would not be useful because _____ . For instance, _____ .

We looked up _____ in the index and found _____ references (on pages _____). When we checked these we felt they would (not) help in our research because _____ . An illustration of this is _____ .

> We then chose to read pages _____ to _____ in detail. These are about _____ .
> We found them (un)helpful for our research because _____ .
> For example _____ .

'**Joss** and I want to find out about **Mount Everest** so we chose this book, called *Mountains.* It was written by **Kenna Bourke** in **2003**.

When we scanned the contents page, headings and pictures, we thought it would be useful because **there was a section in the contents called 'The ascent of Everest', and we found references to Everest all the way through, including two pages about famous people who had climbed it that aren't even mentioned in the contents.**

We looked **Everest** up in the index and found **no** references! **However, we then tried looking up 'Himalayas', which is the mountain range Everest is in, and found seven references (on pages 6, 9, 12, 14, 20, 23 and 44).** When we checked these we felt they would help with our research because **there was information about the Sherpa people who live on Everest, facts about the mountain's height, position, age and rainfall. But it was weird that there were no references to Everest in the index, as there are four pages about it!** An illustration of this is **an interview with Sir Edmund Hillary on page 38 about how he became one of the first two climbers to reach the summit.**

We then chose to read pages **36** to **39** in detail. These are about **famous mountaineers on Everest.** We found them helpful for our research because **they gave information about two important expeditions – Sir John Hunt's expedition when Hillary and Tenzing made it to the top, and an earlier expedition when George Mallory disappeared.** For example, **we learned that some other mountains are more difficult to climb than Everest, but Everest's last 300m of extreme height is what made it Hillary's most challenging peak.**'

Talk about:

- Non-fiction reading skills, including how to appraise the usefulness of a book for research by:
  - scanning contents list, headings, captions, etc.
  - checking keywords in the index
  - checking the age of the book through the copyright date
  - detailed reading of important sections.

- Adjusting the frame according to whether the book is useful or not (cross out *would not* etc. as necessary). Ensure pupils recognise that they must be able to justify all opinions, producing evidence from the text.
- Adjusting the wording of the frame if necessary to fit their evaluation
- The importance of providing examples (and note the different ways of introducing these: *For instance, An illustration is . . . , For example*).
- Ways of ensuring examples are easily to hand during the presentation.

Assessment sheet

Paired presentation

Names _____ Date _____

_____

Preparation	Presentation
collaboration	turn-taking and collaboration
reflecting on content	pace, volume, expression
refining ideas	engagement with audience
note-making	body language
practice	dealing with distractions/problems
Content	**Language**
choice of text	sentence completion and organisation
accuracy/research/evaluation	explicitness
effectiveness	vocabulary
keywords	standard English

Suggestions for the types of behaviour to watch for are given on pages 5, 6 and 8.

Individual presentations

The individual presentations provide opportunities for students to give short sustained talks on their own. We suggest using the paired activities first, to familiarise students with (a) the use of the frames and (b) speaking out to the class, because for some delivering a talk alone is a daunting task.

Preparatory material

Stage 1: In my opinion

These talks provide opportunities for students to state an opinion and argue the case for it. They involve the use of persuasive language, delineation of the individual points in an argument and disguising opinion to seem like fact:

- **There should be a law**: involves explaining an idea, thinking of three arguments to support it, and expressing these as clearly and cogently as possible.
- **The greatest**: involves choosing a personal hero or heroine, providing two reasons why this person is 'the greatest', anticipating a possible objection and refuting it.
- **... should be banned**: involves providing two arguments against an issue, anticipating an objection and refuting it.

These frames specifically cover these aspects of literate talk:

- the language of argument/justifying opinion (e.g. *I have two main reasons ...*);
- connectives to delineate points (e.g. *First of all, Second, Finally*);
- ways of varying expression (e.g. *To begin with, First and foremost, First of all*);
- weasel words that disguise opinion as fact (*clearly, obvious advantage, it is clear that...*);
- conditionals and the subjunctive (e.g. *this law would improve, if this law were passed, other people might argue, perhaps some people would argue*).

Stage 2: Recount

The *Recount* talks provide opportunities for students to give a chronological account couched in more formal, impersonal language than they would usually use. They involve the use of time connectives, conditional language and passive constructions:

- **Autobiography**: involves a chronological account of one's own life so far, singling out specific incidents to illustrate each stage.

- **A great life**: involves choosing a famous person and providing a chronological account of his/her life, explaining why s/he was famous and selecting the most important event.
- **A science experiment**: involves a formal account of a science experiment, using impersonal procedural language.

These frames specifically cover these aspects of literate talk:

- impersonal language including the passive voice (*It was expected*);
- a range of sequential connectives (*Later, Next, Eventually*);
- a range of causal connectives (*As a result, because*);
- a range of ways of showing time passing (*During his/her childhood, As time went on*);
- conditional statements (*perhaps*).

GETTING READY

1. Read the frame and choose a subject you care about. If necessary, spend a little time researching your subject.

2. Read each section of the frame and decide how to finish it. Jot down keywords to remind you. Add extra sentences wherever necessary. Use persuasive language.

3. If it helps you sort out your thoughts, write your presentation out in full. However, the talk must be from memory or brief notes.

4. Practise your presentation, if possible to an audience – they may be able to help you improve it. Practise until you can do it easily.

Introducing individual talks

For each of the activities, give students plenty of time to choose their subject and plan the talk in advance. Each activity makes an ideal homework exercise, but ensure they are well prepared in class beforehand:

- Display enlarged copies of the *Getting Ready* notes and the relevant speaking frame.
- Read and discuss the frame with students. Tell them that, if they wish, they can bring 'visual aids' to help with their talk, such as a picture or poster about their hero, etc.
- Go through the *Getting Ready* notes and demonstrate each stage, modelling the sorts of behaviour and outcomes you want from the students (a completed frame is provided each time).
- When you come to practise the talk, get pupils to 'help' you by reading the sentence starts in chorus.
- Give out copies of the frame for pupils to work on.

Some students may want to compose and write out their entire talk. This is fine, but they should use the frame and notes (or an empty frame and memory) to deliver the talk, not just read a 'prepared speech'.

Some students may want to write and memorise their talk. This is also fine once in a while, as it helps develop auditory memory, but they should also do some talks *ex tempore*.

When observing students' preparation (or assessing/discussing their frames and notes before the talks), watch for the following areas. You could use the assessment sheet on page 42 to focus on the work of some students.

Points to watch for during preparation

Reflecting on content	Does s/he take time to prepare or just rush at it?
Refining ideas	Does s/he draft and edit ideas? Does the talk grow over time?
Note-making	Do notes cover keywords for the presentation? Are they too brief or too wordy?
Practice	Does s/he practise? How – by composing speech as writing? practising to an audience? a mirror?

Points to watch for in content

Choice of subject	Is it a suitable/interesting choice? A genuine choice or any port in a storm?
Accuracy	Is the content factually accurate?
Effectiveness	Is the content interesting? Is there added detail/personal engagement?
Keywords	Are the keywords good ones? Has s/he noted any extra rhetorical devices?

STAGING THE TALK

Think about your audience, not yourself.

- Look at the audience. Talk directly to them. Give them a smile!

- If you have a visual aid, make sure they can see it. Point out anything significant that you mention in the talk.

- Speak slowly and clearly so they can hear. Pause slightly between sections. Speak up – don't mutter.

- If you look confident, the audience will believe in you – and you'll believe in yourself. So stand up straight, don't fidget, look professional!

If anything goes wrong, try to correct it without fuss.

Staging individual presentations

Consider the logistics of fitting everyone's individual presentations into your classroom routine. If students perform in groups of about six, it should be possible to get through the whole class's presentations in a week, devoting five to eight minutes to each. If possible, ensure that the first couple of performers in each batch are fairly fluent readers and speakers. This allows less able students to familiarise themselves with the sentence frames and the sort of vocabulary and sentence patterns that are expected and appreciated.

You may wish to continue the assessment of some students (see page 42), but during performances the teacher should be concentrating on modelling how to listen appreciatively and providing positive feedback. The sheet could be filled in immediately after the presentation, or completed during the presentation by another adult.

Points to watch for in language

Sentence structure	Does s/he use the frame to speak in sentences? Does expression indicate awareness of grammatical boundaries (e.g. commas)? Are any extra sentences framed correctly?
Persuasion and argument	Is the language appropriate to the task? Are the arguments well expressed? Does s/he use any extra persuasive devices (e.g. rhetorical questions, appeals to the audience's emotions)?
Vocabulary	Is vocabulary varied or repetitive? Has s/he used precise nouns, suitable adjectives and verbs?
Coherence	Are there many intrusive 'ands'? Are conditional verb forms used consistently?
Standard English	Has s/he used the vocabulary and grammar of standard English?

Points to watch for in presentation

Pace	Is delivery too fast or too slow?
Voice	Is speech audible? Is the voice expressive or monotonous? Does persuasive language sound suitably persuasive?
Audience engagement	Does s/he address the audience, maintaining eye contact?
Body language	Does s/he stand confidently or self-consciously? Does s/he make good use of any visual aid? Does s/he fidget?
Dealing with problems	Is s/he easily distracted? If anything goes wrong does s/he deal with it satisfactorily?

After thanking each student for his/her contribution, give **at least one piece of positive feedback** such as:

- *I liked the way you used the frame/adjusted the frame to your needs.*
- *That was a very thoughtful speech – you really made me think about the issue.*
- *I was impressed by the way you gave that extra interesting detail about...*

Be very careful in giving negative feedback, as too much criticism could put shy students off speaking up. Focus on the difficulties you had as a listener, rather than those of the student as a speaker, helping him/her recognise what is important in being heard and understood:

- *Could you give your first argument again – I didn't quite understand it.*
- *Could you tell me more about...? I can't imagine it yet.*
- *Could you say the last bit a little slower – I didn't quite catch it.*

THERE SHOULD BE A LAW

In my opinion, there should be a law that _____
_____
_____ .

This law would improve the quality of our lives in
several ways. To begin with, it is clear that _____
_____
_____ .

Another obvious advantage of my law would be _____
_____
_____ .

Finally, most people would agree that if this law were
passed, _____
_____
_____ .

I urge you to support my law!

'In my opinion, there should be a law that **teachers should get one year off teaching every seven years. This 'sabbatical year' would be on full pay, and the teacher would be expected to use it to improve his or her professionalism in some way.**

This law would improve the quality of our lives in several ways. To begin with, it is clear that **teaching is a very taxing and tiring profession. Just imagine being responsible for the education of so many students day in, day out! How long can someone do this job before they drop of exhaustion? If teachers were given regular breaks to recharge their batteries, they would be far better equipped to teach the rest of the time.**

Another obvious advantage of my law would be **that by improving their professionalism, they would become better teachers, with more to offer to their classes. They might use the sabbatical year for study, or research, or travel – and they'd return bubbling with ideas and enthusiasm. The quality of education in this country would soar.**

Finally, most people would agree that if this law were passed, **schools would become much happier places! Teachers wouldn't be tired, they'd have lots of new ideas, and they'd always have the next sabbatical to look forward to … Can you imagine how cheery and bright they'd all be? And happy teachers mean happy students!**

I urge you to support my new law!'

Talk about:

- Choosing a new law. Suggest a few areas that students may be familiar with, such as:

children's rights	animal rights	education
antisocial behaviour	broadcasting	consumers' rights

- Thinking about and around the issue: making sure you can think of three arguments in favour of it.
- How to explain and justify, using explicit organised sentences.
- The use of language in the frame to ensure that the three points are clearly delineated.
- Persuasive devices they might use, e.g.:

  - rhetorical questions, e.g. *How long can someone do this job … ?*
  - emotive language, e.g. *exhaustion, bubbling with ideas, quality of education would soar*
  - expressions that 'turn opinion into fact', e.g. *It is clear that, another obvious advantage*
  - drawing audience along with you, e.g. *most people would agree that …*

At the end of each group of presentations, you could:

- invite questions or further points from the audience;
- hold a vote for the most popular law.

■ *In my opinion*

THE GREATEST

In my opinion, the greatest person who ever lived
is/was _____
_____ .

There are two main points I want to make in support
of this claim. First and foremost, _____
_____
_____ .

Secondly, _____
_____
_____ .

Other people might argue that _____
_____ ,
but I think they are wrong because _____
_____ .

I hope you will agree that _____ has
done more for the world than anyone else in history.

'In my opinion the greatest person who ever lived was **William Shakespeare, the Elizabethan playwright.**

There are two main points I want to make in support of this claim. First and foremost, **Shakespeare's plays are brilliant and timeless. Have you ever thought how amazing it is that they are just as popular now as they were more than four hundred years ago? And they were just as popular in Charles II's time, and Victoria's, and every generation. Not only that, but they are loved and performed in every country of the world, from America to Africa to China. Think how memorable his characters are – Macbeth, Hamlet, Romeo and Juliet. And how brilliantly he used language to bring them to life. No other artist has touched the hearts and minds of so many people.**

Secondly, **Shakespeare's contribution to the English language is greater than any other human being's. So many of the expressions we use every day come from his pen. He contributed countless words to the dictionary (incidentally 'countless' was one of his) and helped to make the English language into an international treasure. Consider the many great writers this country has produced since Shakespeare! Dickens, Austen, J K Rowling! Shakespeare unlocked the language, and it's there for all of us to use. And now English is the international language, our greatest gift to the world. I believe that Shakespeare did more than anyone to make English what it is today.**

Other people might argue that **a playwright is not as important as a doctor, or a prophet, or a politician,** but I think they are wrong because **through his plays, Shakespeare helps to form people's minds. He can explain to us who we are and why we are like that – and his understanding is universal.**

I hope you will agree that **William Shakespeare** has done more for the world than anyone else in history.'

Talk about:

- Choosing a hero or heroine. Some students may want to choose a pop star or sporting hero. This is fine as long as they can provide arguments and state the case with enough conviction.
- How to explain and justify, using explicit organised sentences.
- The use of language in the frame to ensure that the three points are clearly delineated (you could compare this with the language of *There Should Be A Law* to demonstrate alternative constructions).
- Persuasive devices they might use, e.g.:

  - rhetorical questions, e.g. *Have you ever thought…?*
  - emotive language, e.g. *brilliant, timeless, memorable*
  - expressions that 'turn opinion into fact', e.g. *No other artist has…*
  - appealing to the audience along with imperative verbs, e.g. *Think how… Consider …*

At the end of each group of presentations, you could:

- invite questions or further points from the audience;
- hold a vote for the most popular hero.

■ In my opinion

. . . SHOULD BE BANNED

In my opinion, _____ should be banned.

I have two main reasons for believing this. First of all, as I'm sure you'll agree, _____ _____ .

My second important reason for wanting to ban _____ is that _____ _____ .

Perhaps some people would argue that _____ _____ . However, I would point out that _____ _____ .

It is clear that a ban on _____ would be a great step forward, _____ .

'In my opinion, **junk mail** should be banned.

I have two main reasons for believing this. First of all, as I'm sure you'll agree, **it is a great waste of money. Apart from the stamp, there's the cost of the paper and printing – a single item of junk mail probably costs about 50p to produce. Think about how many 50ps that is, when they send their stupid letters to thousands of people. And have you ever thought about how all this is paid for? Why – by us, the customers! The costs of advertising are added to the costs of goods and services, so if there were no junk mail lots of things would be cheaper!**

My second important reason for wanting to ban **junk mail** is that **it is terribly wasteful of paper. Vast numbers of trees must be cut down to make enough paper for all the junk mail in the world, and then it's just thrown into people's bins, sometimes without even being opened. Surely we should be conserving our planet, not destroying it to create something completely pointless!**

Perhaps some people would argue that **junk mail keeps you informed about things you might want to buy.** However, I would point out that **it's better to have the exercise of going to the shops and seeing what's available. Even if you're too lazy to do that, access to the web means we can now search for anything we want, exactly to our specifications.**

It is clear that a ban on **junk mail** would be a great step forward, **for consumers, for tired postmen and for the planet!**'

Talk about:

- Choosing something to ban. Suggest a few possible contenders, such as:

homework	school uniform	school
football	cabbage	government interference in education

- Thinking about and around the issue: making sure you can think of three arguments in favour of it.
- How to explain and justify, using explicit organised sentences.
- The use of language in the frame to ensure that the three points are clearly delineated (you could compare it with the language of *There Should Be A Law* and *The Greatest* to demonstrate alternative constructions).
- Persuasive devices they might use, e.g.:

  - rhetorical questions, e.g. *Have you ever thought ... ?*
  - emotive language, e.g. *stupid letter, vast numbers of trees*
  - drawing audience along with you, e.g. *I'm sure you'll agree, surely, you must agree.*

At the end of each group of presentations, you could:

- invite questions or further points from the audience;
- hold a vote for the item they'd most like to ban.

36

■ Recount

AUTOBIOGRAPHY

My name is _____ , I am _____ years old, and this is the story of my life so far.

I was born on _____ in _____ .
As a baby, I _____ .
Perhaps the most significant event of my early life was _____ .

I started school at the age of _____ and my first memory is of _____ .
Since then, I've been in _____ classes, _____ _____ .

The most vivid memory of my school career is _____ _____ .

When I was _____ .
This was an important event in my life because _____ .

The most amusing thing that has ever happened to me was _____ .

© 2011 Sue Palmer, *Speaking Frames: How to Teach Talk for Writing: Ages 10–14*. London: Routledge.

'My name is **Michael Burton,** I am **13** years old, and this is the story of my life so far.

I was born on **28 May 1998** in **Manchester, England.** As a baby, **I was apparently rather noisy and not a very good sleeper. My mum says I squawked practically all the time and she didn't get a proper night's sleep for two years!** Perhaps the most significant event of my early life was **moving house when I was two. We moved up to Scotland and have lived here ever since. I don't remember anything about Manchester at all.**

I started school at the age of **five** and my first memory is of **drinking my milk through a straw. The other boys and I used to have a competition to see who could make the most noise when we were draining the bottle.** Since then I've been in **five** classes, **three at my primary school in Yairfoot, and two here at Borders High in Galashiels. At Borders my form tutors have been Mr Marks and Miss McLelland.**

The most vivid memory of my school career is **the day I started at Borders High. Yairfoot is a really small school, so I was worried about all the people, but as soon as I arrived I met a boy with red hair and a big grin who'd been on the transition day with me. His name is Alex Sanders and we've been best friends ever since.**

When I was **five, my little brother James was born.** This was an important event in my life because **I wasn't the youngest in the family any more. Also I thought they'd sent me to school to get rid of me so he could take over. This was quite hard for a five-year-old to cope with, so I did try to murder Jimmy several times. However, my parents worked out what was going on, and talked me round.**

The most amusing thing that ever happened to me was **when Alex's dog Nellie accidentally fell into a pond. She's a Basset hound and they have these big long ears. She stepped on some pondweed, thinking it was solid ground, and just stood there stupidly as she sank. When she went underwater, for some reason her ears spread out on either side and floated. I'll never forget her bewildered look as she went down. Or the pondweed all over Alex when he'd pulled her out.**'

Talk about:

- The organisation of the talk: introduction; babyhood; school; important event; amusing event.
- The possibility of using some visual aids (photographs, a poster, maybe even a home video) to illustrate the talk.
- The importance of ensuring each sentence of the talk doesn't begin with 'I'. Note the many ways in the frame of avoiding this.
- How extra detail makes the talk more interesting. Pupils should feel free to add to the frame, and to elaborate on any part.

■ Recount

A GREAT LIFE

_____ lived in _____*(place)*_____, about _____ years ago. S/He is famous because _____ _____ .

_____ was born in the year _____ . During his/her childhood _____ .

Later, in ___*(year)*___ , s/he _____ _____ .

Perhaps the most significant event in _____ 's life occurred in _____*(year)*_____ , when _____ _____ . As a result, _____ .

As time went on, _____ _____ .

_____ died in ___*(year)*___ at the age of _____ but will always be remembered as _____ .

'**Elizabeth I** lived in **England,** about **450** years ago. She is famous because **she was the daughter of King Henry VIII, and when he died she became Queen of England.**

Elizabeth was born in the year **1533.** During her childhood, **she was looked after by a number of stepmothers. Her own mother, Anne Boleyn, was executed by Henry VIII when Elizabeth was a baby. He wanted to get rid of her so he could marry someone else and have a son – Anne had only given him a girl. Imagine how terrible it must be that your father executes your mother, especially when it seems your fault for being the wrong gender!**

Later, in **1558**, she **became Queen. Her younger brother Edward and her older sister Mary had both died, and she was Henry's only remaining child. She was a very clever woman, and ruled England sensibly and well. During her reign England produced many great poets, including William Shakespeare. There were also famous sailors and discoverers like Sir Walter Raleigh, who first brought tobacco and potatoes to England. Elizabeth encouraged her people to achieve great things, and they all loved her and called her Good Queen Bess.**

Perhaps the most significant event in **Elizabeth**'s life occurred in **1588,** when **a great Armada of ships from Spain came to attack England. Elizabeth dressed in armour and went to the docks where her armies were gathered and gave a famous speech to inspire them.** As a result, **her people loved her even more, especially when the Spanish Armada was destroyed.**

As time went on, **Elizabeth grew old and started to wear red wigs to cover up the fact she was grey. She also wore thick white makeup on her face, and lots of bright jewels and rich clothes so that she would still look impressive and inspire her people.**

Elizabeth died in **1603** at the age of **70,** but will always be remembered as **a great queen and leader of her people.**'

Talk about:

- Choice of 'great life': they must be dead, and it's best to choose someone you admire or find very interesting.
- The importance of research to ensure your talk is factually correct.
- The possibility of using visual aids: pictures, posters, etc..
- The order of the talk: introduction, childhood, adulthood, key event (think hard how you're going to select this), later life, death and conclusion.
- The importance of detail and interesting anecdotes to keep your audience's attention.

■ Recount

A SCIENCE EXPERIMENT

This is an account of an experiment to see _____ _____ .

The equipment required was _____ _____ .

The procedure was as follows: _____ _____ .

Explain the procedure using time connectives, e.g.

First ... Next ...
Then ... Meanwhile ...
Eventually ...

impersonal language and the passive voice, e.g.

were placed ...
were observed ...
was noted ...

It was expected that _____ .

Our findings were that _____ .

This suggests that _____ .

'This is an account of an experiment to see **whether evaporation of water is affected by the temperature.**

The equipment required was **three squares of thick card (all the same size), three plastic trays, a stopwatch, a digital thermometer and a bucket of water.**

The procedure was as follows: **first, the squares of card were all dipped in the bucket for ten seconds, to ensure they absorbed the same amount of water. They were placed in the plastic trays, and kept at different temperatures: one in the bottom of a fridge, one in a cool outdoor shed and the third in a warm room. The temperature of each location was checked with the digital thermometer. Then the cards were checked at ten minute intervals to see if they were dry.**

It was expected that **the card in the warm position would dry first.**

Our findings were that **the card kept in the warm classroom (22°C) dried after 40 minutes; the card in the cool shed (11°C) took 3 hours 50 minutes to dry, and the card in the refrigerator (2°C) was still wet after six hours.**

This suggests that **temperature affects the speed at which water evaporates – the warmer it is the faster evaporation occurs.'**

Talk about:

- Bringing information from science lessons to the English classroom (this may require some negotiation with the science department).
- Choosing an experiment: this activity might be best conducted at intervals throughout the term, allowing different students to recount different experiments from science lessons.
- Use of the passive voice: this is best taught orally. Give students short sentences in the active to translate into the passive (e.g. *James ate the orange; The man wrote a letter; Romans wore togas; The Normans invaded Britain in 1066*). Some students will catch on quickly – let them model the procedure, so that other students gradually get the idea. Then ask students who are proficient to provide similarly constructed sentences (subject – verb – object) that others can try twiddling into the passive. Plenty of this sort of oral practice is much better than trying to teach 'rules' or practising passive constructions through writing.
- The business of formal writing – nowadays many science experiments are written in the active voice, but the passive still lingers in many texts students will have to read. Go through and point out all the passive constructions before they try the activity.

Assessment sheet

Individual presentation

Name _____ Date _____

Preparation	Presentation
approach to planning	use of speaking frame
reflecting on content	pace, volume, expression
refining ideas	engagement with audience
note-making	body language
practice	dealing with distractions/problems
Content	**Language**
choice of topic	sentence structure and coherence
accuracy/research	language use (e.g. rhetorical devices)
effectiveness	vocabulary
keywords	standard English

Suggestions for the types of behaviour to watch for are given on pages 26 and 28.

Group presentations

Group presentations provide opportunities for two sorts of talk:

- collaborative talk within the group around the specific task – talk for learning;
- participation in the formal presentation using the speaking frame – talk for writing.

Many thinking skills programmes are based on the first type of 'talk for learning': small group, open-ended discussion, in which students share and build on each other's ideas. The ideal size for a group seems to be about five or six. Certainly there should be no more than six in a group.

However, for group discussion to be successful, students need preliminary work to establish procedures and rules for behaviour. They should by now be familiar with speaking frames and how to use them, so the emphasis in the introduction to these group activities is on developing (or revising) the ground rules of discussion. This discussion will involve decision making, generating ideas and sharing out sections for the eventual presentation. The final formal presentation is a further opportunity to familiarise students with literate language patterns.

The activities are designed to provide opportunities for shared creative thinking, involving:

- generating and evaluating ideas;
- explaining and justifying ideas;
- discussing, arguing a case and reaching agreement.

The final presentation involves shared responsibility, formal turn-taking, and speaking in 'literate language'. While the group provides support, each student has an individual responsibility for their part in the performance, e.g. speaking clearly, adopting an appropriate speed and volume.

Preparatory material

Stage 1: Compare and contrast

The frames specifically cover these aspects of literate talk:

- speaking in complete sentences, varying sentence construction;
- ways of introducing a number of non-sequential points (*The first ... Another ... A further ... Finally*);
- varying expression (*similar, alike, both, have in common*);
- explanatory and justificatory language.

Stage 2: Points of view

The frames specifically cover these aspects of literate talk:

- speaking in complete complex sentences, varying sentence construction;
- ways of introducing a number of points of view, on both sides of an argument (e.g. *Some people believe . . . On the other hand . . .*);
- varying expression (e.g. *supporters, in favour of; opponents, critics*);
- conditional language (e.g. *probably, could be claimed, might, always the chance that*)
- explanatory and justificatory language;
- formal language (e.g. *Moreover, After consideration*) including the passive (e.g. *it could be claimed . . . an argument often put . . .*).

RULES FOR GROUP DISCUSSION

Listen to others:

- look at the speaker;
- consider the point they are making;
- don't interrupt;
- ask for further information if necessary.

Make sure everyone gets a chance to speak:

- shy people – be brave!
- bold people – don't hog the floor!

Always be polite – especially when you disagree.

Give reasons for what you say, e.g.:

- 'I disagree because ...'
- 'I think ... because ...'

There are no wrong answers – just steps towards a solution.

Take turns to be secretary and make notes.

Introducing group discussion

Before asking students to work in groups on a specific task, spend time establishing the ground rules for behaviour. Ideally, students should devise these for themselves through class discussion, thus ensuring they have ownership of – and therefore greater commitment to – the final list. However, through guiding discussion, ensure they cover all the points listed opposite.

Ensure you establish the rules firmly through class discussion, before asking the pupils to work in groups. Remember always to model the desired behaviour yourself during class discussion.

To introduce the activities:

- Display your *Rules for Group Discussion* and an enlarged copy of the relevant speaking frame.
- Read the frame with students. Discuss what is involved (see boxes below) and how the group might organise itself to create the presentation.
- Give a small copy of the frame to each group.

You could use the assessment sheet on page 62 to focus on the work of one or two groups.

Points to watch for during preparation

Collaboration	Are they working as a team? How did they allocate/share tasks? Is anyone left out or too dominant?
Reflecting on content	Is there genuine discussion, reflecting on content?
Refining ideas	Are they building on each other's ideas, making improvements?
Note-making	Do notes cover keywords for the presentation? Is the secretarial system working? Is each student involved in making the notes for his/her section?
Practice	Do they use practice to improve content and presentation? Do they give useful feedback to each other?

Points to watch for in content

Creativity	How did they generate ideas? Are ideas too off the wall or too stuck in the mud? Are they open-minded about all contributions?
Choice of ideas	How did they agree which ideas to use? Were the choices the best ones or too much influenced by populist group dynamics?
Effectiveness	Can they explain ideas clearly, and find arguments to justify them?
Keywords	Are they choosing good keywords – precise nouns and noun phrases, powerful adjectives and verbs?

Give positive specific feedback as for paired work on page 5.

GIVING THE TALK

1. Make sure you know who is going to say each section. Stand in the right order.

2. Don't waste time between speakers. Swap quickly, so the presentation flows smoothly.

3. When it's your turn:

    - look at the audience;
    - speak slowly, clearly and with expression;
    - stand and act confidently.

4. When it's not your turn, fade into the background:

    - look down, or at the speaker;
    - don't make any sound;
    - don't do anything that might distract the speaker or audience.

5. If anything goes wrong, work as a team to sort it out.

Staging group presentations

If students are working in groups of six, it should be possible to stage all the presentations in one session. Display an enlarged copy of the *Giving The Talk* notes opposite, and talk through them with students, reminding them about general points they have learned about speaking in public.

Start with an able group, so the less able students have the chance to see a model before performing themselves. Use your feedback to the early groups to help others – if early presentations do not work well, it might be helpful to discuss the problems, and give groups a little longer to prepare.

Points to watch for in language

Sentence structure	Does their delivery indicate awareness of grammatical boundaries? Are any extra sentences framed correctly?
Explicitness and argument	Are the points made explicitly enough? Are explanations and arguments clear?
Vocabulary	Is vocabulary varied or repetitive? Have they used precise nouns, suitable adjectives and verbs?
Standard English	Have they used the vocabulary and grammar of standard English? Is there agreement in terms of tense, person, number?

Points to watch for in presentation

Turn-taking/ collaboration	Is their turn-taking organised or chaotic? Are they working as a group? Is their performance organised or chaotic?
Pace	Is the pace of the presentation/individual speakers satisfactory?
Voice	Is each speaker audible? Are voices expressive or monotonous?
Audience engagement	Do they address the audience or each other? Does their performance engage attention?
Body language	Does each speaker 'hold the floor' confidently? Do non-speakers fade back or attract attention?
Dealing with problems	Are they easily distracted? Do they work as a group to overcome problems?

At the end of each presentation, give brief feedback on key points of the performance, making praise specific wherever possible, e.g.:

- *I especially liked Andy's point because he explained it very clearly.*
- *Your turn-taking was excellent, so the talk flowed smoothly with no disruption between speakers.*
- *I liked the way you enunciated your words so clearly, so we could hear every word.*

Where feedback is negative, give it from the point of view of the audience, e.g.:

- *It was hard to concentrate on what Ben was saying because people were moving behind him.*
- *I didn't always understand your points because the explanations seemed a bit muddled.*
- *I'm afraid you lost me a bit because of the big gaps when you swapped over.*

If you invite the rest of the class to comment on aspects of the performance (perhaps basing it on the *Giving The Talk* notes), ensure the criticism is constructive.

■ Compare and contrast

COMPARE

There are several ways in which _____ and _____ could be said to be similar.

The first way they are alike is that they are both _____ .

Another similarity is that they _____ _____ .

A further feature they have in common is _____ _____ .

Finally, they both _____ _____ .

We think the most significant similarity is that _____ because _____ _____ .

'There are several ways in which **a cup** and **a shoe** could be said to be similar.

The first way they are both alike is that they are both **containers. The cup is a container for liquids and the shoe is a container for someone's foot.**

Another similarity is that they **are man-made objects. Both are manufactured in factories, and sold in shops.**

A further feature they have in common is **that they are small enough to be held in a human hand.**

Finally, they both **need regular cleaning. A cup must be washed after use, and a shoe needs polishing to keep it looking good.**

We think the most significant similarity is that **they are containers,** because **this is their function. Their size, the way they are made, and the need to clean them all depend on their function as containers.'**

For this activity, don't give a choice of items to compare. Present each group with two disparate objects – if possible, give them real things that they can handle and investigate. Coming up with four points of comparison is a useful thinking skills activity, so practically any items will do.

Talk about:

- The importance of explicitness and clarity in explanation and description (remind them of what they learned through the *Tell the Alien* activities).
- The sort of technical language that make descriptions sound 'grown-up' and professional, e.g. *container* as opposed to *holder for something*. Students may find a dictionary or thesaurus helpful in this respect.
- The 'grown up' vocabulary in the frame: *a further feature* (instead of *another thing*) *significant* (instead of *most important*).
- Varying language (e.g. *are similar, are alike, similarity, have in common*).

This frame can be reused – for pairs, individuals or groups – whenever students are required to make comparisons, e.g. comparing characters, settings and plots in literature.

■ Compare and contrast

CONTRAST

A _____ and _____ are different in a number of ways.

First of all, _____ but _____
_____ .

Another difference is that _____,
while _____ .

Thirdly, _____ in contrast to _____ which _____ .

Finally, _____ , but _____
_____ .

We think the most significant difference between them is _____ because _____
_____ .

'A **cup** and **a shoe** are different in a number of ways.

First of all, **a cup is used for containing liquid,** but **a shoe is used for containing someone's foot.**

Another difference is that **a cup is usually made of china clay** while **a shoe is usually made of leather, fabric or plastic. Cups can also be made of plastic, but it is a different sort of plastic.**

Thirdly, **shoes have to be fairly flexible to allow the wearer's foot to move about,** in contrast to **cups** which **are more rigid. If they were too flexible, the liquid might slosh about and spill out.**

Finally, **you wash cups in soapy water,** but **shoes are generally cleaned with a cloth and polish. If you washed leather shoes in soapy water, it would not do them any good at all.**

We think the most significant difference between them is **the material they are made from,** because **that affects other properties, like flexibility and washability.'**

Again, don't give a choice of items. Give the group two objects – they could be real objects to handle, or just named objects, places, characters. Coming up with four points of contrast is another useful thinking skills activity.

Talk about:

- The importance of explicitness and clarity in explanation and description (remind them of what they learned through the *Tell the Alien* activities).
- The use of the weasel word *usually* to make a generalised statement.
- The sort of technical language that make descriptions sound 'grown-up' and professional, e.g. *flexible* as opposed to *bendy*. Pupils may find a dictionary or thesaurus helpful in this respect.
- The 'grown-up' vocabulary in the frame: *in contrast to, significant*, varying language (e.g. *are different, difference, in contrast to*).

This frame can be reused – by individuals, pairs or groups – whenever pupils have to look for differences, e.g. *the difference between a play script and a story, the differences between certain text types.*

■ Compare and contrast

COMPARE AND CONTRAST

In some ways, _____ and _____ are alike. For instance, they are both _____ .

Another feature they have in common is that _____ _____ .

Furthermore, they both _____ .

However, they also differ in some ways. For example, _____ , while _____ .

Another difference is that _____ whereas _____ .

Finally, _____ but _____ .

On the whole, the similarities/differences seem more significant than the similarities/differences because _____ .

'In some ways, **dogs** and **cats** are alike. For instance, they are both **four-legged animals.**

Another feature they have in common is that **they can both be domesticated and kept as pets.**

Furthermore, they are both **carnivorous.**

However they also differ is some ways. For example, **dogs like to please their owners and to be with them whenever possible,** while **cats tend to live their own life, and only bother with their owners when they feel like it.**

Another difference is that **dogs usually have to be taken out for exercise and kept on a lead,** whereas **cats come and go as they please, and don't need anyone to go with them.**

Finally, **dogs bark and whine,** but **cats meow and purr.**

On the whole, the similarities seem more significant than the differences because **they are more fundamental. The differences are just little things, but being a four-legged carnivorous domesticated animal is very particular.'**

Again, don't give a choice of items. For this activity, you could choose any objects, places or people for each group to compare and contrast.

Talk about:

- The importance of explicitness and clarity in explanation and description (remind them of what they learned through the *Tell the Alien* activities).
- The use of the weasel word *usually* to make a generalised statement.
- The sort of technical language that make descriptions sound 'grown-up' and professional, e.g. *flexible* as opposed to *bendy*. Pupils may find a dictionary or thesaurus helpful in this respect.
- The 'grown-up' vocabulary in the frame: *in contrast to, significant*, varying language (e.g. *are different, difference, in contrast to*).

This frame can be reused – by individuals, pairs or groups – whenever pupils have to look for differences, e.g. *the difference between a playscript and a story, the differences between certain text types.*

■ Points of view

A GREAT DEBATE

There is a great deal of debate about whether _____
_____ .

Some people believe that _____
_____ . They argue that _____
_____ .

However, other people claim that _____
_____ .

Another argument often put in favour of _____
is that _____ .

On the other hand, it could be said that _____
_____ .

Supporters of _____ point out that
_____ , while opponents reply that ____
_____ .

On the whole, we think we agree with supporters/
critics that _____ .

There is a great deal of debate about **whether cars should be allowed into the centre of town.**

Some people believe that **banning cars would improve the quality of life in the town for everyone.** They argue that **the current problems with congestion and parking are making life miserable for shoppers and office workers. We need to give the streets back to the people.**

However, other people claim that **banning cars would mean the death of the town centre. If shoppers couldn't bring their cars into town they'd go somewhere else. There would be more out of town shopping centres, and people would go there instead. The town centre shops would go out of business.**

Another argument often put in favour of **banning cars** is that **we could have a cheap park and ride scheme from the outskirts of town, so that shoppers could be brought in and out by bus. This would combine the convenience of an out of town shopping centre with all the advantages of a proper town centre.**

On the other hand, it could be said that **most people don't like relying on public transport. They want to be able to take their cars near to the shops so that they don't have to carry their shopping so far. Unless the park and ride was very frequent, people would get fed up of waiting for it.**

Supporters of **a car-free town centre** point out that **it would also be safer for pedestrians,** while opponents reply that **if we ban cars there would soon be hardly any pedestrians left, because shoppers would go elsewhere.**

On the whole, we think we agree with critics that **people love their cars so much, they wouldn't come to town if they couldn't drive here. Instead of banning cars, we have to look at ways of improving parking and reorganising the one way system to avoid congestion.**

Talk about:

● Possible areas of debate. Suggest a few obvious ones such as:

    homework   school uniform   hunting

but also suggest areas that students may be familiar with, such as:

    children's rights   animal rights   education
    antisocial behaviour   broadcasting   consumers' rights.

● Thinking about and around the issue: making sure you can think of three arguments in favour and three against.
● How to explain and justify, using explicit organised sentences.
● The use of language in the frame to ensure that the points (and the two points of view) are clearly delineated.

■ Points of view

ORDER OF IMPORTANCE

_____ , _____, _____, _____ and _____ are/were all _____ .

After consideration, we think that the most important of the five is/was probably _____ because _____ .

However, there is also a good case for _____ , which/who is important because _____ _____ .

Moreover, it could be claimed that _____ is/was very significant, as _____ .

At the other extreme, we agreed _____ was not high in the order. Our main reason for this was _____ .

Finally, we felt _____ should come last. This was because _____ .

The most difficult choice was between _____ and _____ because _____ .

Shakepeare, J. K. Rowling, Roald Dahl, Stephanie Meyer and **Anne Fine** are all **authors.**

After consideration, we think that the most important of the five was probably **Shakespeare** because **his plays are famous all over the world, and have been famous for 400 years. This probably makes him the most important and influential writer of all time.**

However, there is also a good case for **J. K. Rowling,** who is important because **she is also world famous and has probably sold as many books as Shakespeare even though she has only been writing for about 15 years. She has made more money out of writing than any of the others.**

Moreover, it could be claimed that **Anne Fine** is very significant, **as her books are always thought provoking and well written. As well as her writing she has always worked hard to promote reading, including being the Children's Laureate.**

At the other extreme, we agreed **Roald Dahl** was not high in the order. Our main reason for this was **that his books are not serious. Shakespeare, J. K. Rowling and Anne Fine all write books that make you think, but Roald Dahl's stories are just entertainment.**

Finally, we felt **Stephanie Meyer** should come last. This was because **her books are good reads but not very memorable. We think that all the other writers will be remembered for a long time, but Stephanie Meyer will soon be forgotten.**

The most difficult choice was between **Roald Dahl** and **Anne Fine** because **Roald Dahl is more popular and we think his books will last. We were not sure that Anne Fine's books will last that long, even though they are probably better books. In the end, we decided that Anne Fine's other work for literature won her the higher place.**

It is probably best to define the discussion areas, e.g.:

- people – famous people from history, entertainers, poets, sporting heroes, etc.
- books/films/TV programmes/poems, etc.
- places – holiday resorts, cities, local amenities, etc.
- activities – school subjects, occupations, etc.
- other – tools, foodstuffs, plants, animals, famous events from history, etc..

Talk about:

- choosing five people, places, items to discuss: each member of the group could choose one and pitch their case, after which they vote on the best five;
- adjusting the frame to the subject – cross out inappropriate alternatives (e.g. *was/were*);
- the importance of having good reasons for your choices (give as many as possible for each choice – add extra sentences to the frame if necessary);
- how to explain and justify choices, using explicit organised sentences;
- the use of language in the frame to ensure that the five points are clearly delineated.

■ Points of view

WHAT IF?

Our group debated whether the world would be a better or worse place if _____ .

On the one hand, we felt this change might make life better because _____ .

A further benefit could be _____ .

There is also the possibility that _____ .

On the other hand, if _____ , there might be problems due to _____ .

There is always the chance that _____ .

In the worst case scenario, _____ .

Having weighed up all the possibilities, we've concluded that _____
_____ .

'Our group debated whether the world would be a better or worse place if **there were no such thing as money.**

On the one hand, we felt this change might make life better because**, as the Bible says,** *the love of money is the root of all evil.* **We think that most of the bad things that happen in the world are caused by people trying to get more money.**

A further benefit could be **that without money, people would be valued for what they are like and what they can do, not for how much money and how many possessions they have.**

There is also the possibility that **in a world without money, everything would be shared out more equally, and people could live in peace.**

On the other hand, **if there were no money,** there might be problems due to **how people would get the things they wanted. It is all very well to say that they would swap with other people, but sometimes the other people nearby might not have what you want to swap. There would be no way of developing a trading system.**

There is always the chance that, **in a moneyless world, the human race might not have developed, because without trade the world would not have moved on. There would probably be no civilisation – and that means no industry, no TV, no comfortable homes …**

In the worst case scenario, **in this uncivilised world, the most strong and powerful people might take advantage of everyone else and turn them into slaves.**

Having weighed up all the possibilities, we've concluded that **money is probably a good thing. The Bible doesn't say that** *money is the root of evil,* **but** *the love of money.* **That means that people should use money, but not want it for its own sake. If we do that we get the best of both worlds.**

Talk about:

- Possible areas of discussion. These could be philosophical questions, as in the example above, or hypothetical questions about current areas of study ('What if Henry VIII had had three sons?') or related to pupils' own interests ('What if the internet were available free on every mobile?'). Ask pupils for ideas to create a list of 'what if' questions from which groups can select.
- The importance of talking around the question, and developing ideas, to ensure that you have three good points for and three arguments against.
- Conditional language (*might, could, would, possibly, probably* – see page 73) including the use of the subjunctive (*if there **were** no money*).
- The importance of explicit language to explain and justify each point.

Assessment sheet

Group presenation

Group members _____

_____ Date _____

Preparation	Presentation
collaboration	*turn-taking and collaboration*
reflecting on content	*pace, volume, expression*
refining ideas	*engagement with audience*
note-making	*body language*
practice	*dealing with distractions/problems*
Content	**Language**
creativity	*sentence structure*
choice of ideas	*explicitness and argument*
effectiveness	*vocabulary*
keywords	*standard English*

Suggestions for the types of behaviour to watch for are given on pages 46 and 48.

Signpost smorgasbord

These frames introduce common 'literate language' constructions for expressing key ideas (and the interrelationships between ideas) which students will meet in literacy lessons and across the curriculum.

The frames familiarise students with the vocabulary and structure of literate language through the opportunity to 'play around' with useful constructions orally. As well as introducing them to these language patterns (for both writing and speaking) the activities should help develop thinking and communication skills in general, as access to suitable language can facilitate thought.

A lesson plan is provided for introducing each frame, although teachers may find that opportunities to use them crop up naturally in literacy lessons or other areas of the curriculum. Elements from the frames may also be used to create specific speaking frames for further paired, individual or group activities.

Illustrating punctuation

When using the speaking frames, ensure students are aware of punctuation (and its relationship to oral expression) by the use of visual symbols. Devise signals to represent commas and full stops, e.g.:

- comma – draw a large comma shape in the air with a finger;
- full stop – jab the air with a finger.

Always use these when demonstrating the frames and ask students to use them when feeding back to the class.

Listen – imitate – innovate – invent

Some of the smorgasbord pages contain frames which have appeared in the first *Speaking Frames* book. Since a key element of the listen – imitate – innovate – invent system is the importance of repetition, important constructions need to be rehearsed regularly. However, all the pages have been updated, usually by the addition of more complex vocabulary or constructions.

CAUSE AND EFFECT

When ...., _____

If ...., _____

..............................., so _____

.... This causes _____

.... This means that _____

.... This results in _____

.... As a result, _____

.... Therefore _____

_____ because ....

The reason _____ is that..............................

_____ due to ....

Cause and effect frames are included in both *Speaking Frames* books because the constructions involved are so important. However, the page in this book contains three frames which do not appear in Book 1. Students who have played with these frames in earlier years will need no introduction and can go straight to using them to express their own cause and effect sentences. They may need their attention drawn to the three constructions in which there is a change to the verb form.

Introductory lesson

- Introduce the terms *cause* and *effect* and ensure students know what they mean. Point out that in the frames:

  Cause = ... Effect = _____

- Illustrate by completing the first frame using a cause/effect that is either:

  - obvious (**When** the window is open, it is cold)
  - silly (**When** it is raining, Miss X turns into a parrot).

  Indicate the point where the comma separates the two chunks by drawing a large comma in the air with your finger.
- Ask students to fill the same cause and effect into the next six frames, indicating the comma in the same way.

  - **If** it is raining, Miss X turns into a parrot.
  - It is raining, **so** Miss X turns into a parrot.
  - It is raining. **This causes** Miss X to turn into a parrot. (Note change in verb form.)
  - It is raining. **This means** Miss X turns into a parrot.
  - It is raining. **This results in** Miss X turning into a parrot. (Note change in verb form.)
  - It is raining. **Therefore** Miss X turns into a parrot.

- Point out that sometimes, the effect is stated before the cause:

  - Miss X turns into a parrot **because** it is raining.
  - **The reason** Miss X turns into a parrot **is that** it is raining.
  - Miss X has turned into a parrot **due to** the rain. (Note change in verb form.)

- You may wish to point out that in the first two frames, the chunks can be reversed:

  - Miss X turns into a parrot **when** it is raining.
  - Miss X turns into a parrot **if** it is raining.

- Ask students in pairs to think up their own cause and effect and take turns to fit it into the frames (remind them of the verb changes with *This causes, This results in* and *due to*). Ask a number of students to feed back their results to the class, starting with more able students, so that the less able hear the model a few times before trying it themselves.

SEQUENCE OF EVENTS

Firstly, _____   Secondly, _____   Finally, _____

First of all _____   Next _____

Eventually, _____

To start with _____   After that _____

At last, _____

To begin with _____   Later _____

At the end, _____

When _____ , _____   Since _____ , _____

After _____ , _____   Before _____ , _____

Until _____ , _____

While _____ , _____   As _____ , _____

Meanwhile _____

This exercise is useful preparation for fiction writing, or cross-curricular writing of recount, instruction or explanation text. These constructions have been introduced in earlier books, but need frequent revisiting to ensure students have a wide range of 'sequencing signposts'.

Introductory lesson

- Introduce the term *sequence of events* and ensure students know what it means. Point out that:

  - the words in the first column are ways of starting a sequence;
  - those in the second are for the middle of a sequence;
  - the last column has words that can conclude a sequence.

  Any word can be chosen from any column so there are many possible permutations, e.g.:

  > *First . . .*   *After that . . .*   *In the end . . .*

  However, certain forms of words are sometimes more appropriate than others, depending on the sentence.

- Illustrate writing a sequence of three events on the board, e.g. Wednesday morning school up to break time: *We go for registration. We have a maths lesson. We go out for break.* Then select three suitable words or phrases from the lists and say the sentences with them in place:

  > **First of all** *we go for registration.* **Next** *we have a maths lesson.*
  > **Finally***, we go out for break.*

  Indicate any commas by drawing them in the air with your finger.

- Ask students to try alternative words and phrases, discussing whether they 'sound right'.

- Point out that, in sequences of more than three events, you can use extra connectives from the central column, avoiding repetition (one *Then* is fine; more than one sounds dreary). Add in another event:

  > **First of all** *we go for registration.* **Next** *we have a maths lesson.* **Later** *we have half an hour's English.* **Finally***, we go out for break.*

- Demonstrate that the constructions beneath the lines can be used anywhere:

  > **When** *school starts, we go for registration.*
  > **After** *register, we have a maths lesson.*
  > **Next** *comes half an hour's English* **until** *the bell goes for break.*

- Ask students in pairs to think up a simple sequence of events, e.g. things you do when you get up in the morning/when you get home from school/when you eat your packed lunch. They should then try expressing it in as many different ways as possible, varying connectives to achieve different effects. If they note down each sequence of connectives, some pairs can feed back their efforts to the rest of the class.

ADDING INFORMATION

as well   too

Also ...

Furthermore ...

Moreover ...

In addition, ...

What is more ...

A second/third reason is ...

Another point is ...

A further argument is ...

Finally, ...

The first *Speaking Frames* book introduces a limited number of ways a speaker or writer can add to information. This activity builds on these, and includes constructions for adding point on point, argument on argument, and reason on reason. This is such a common requirement in writing and speech that students' language use benefits enormously if they have a range of constructions available (instead of the ubiquitous *and*).

Introductory lesson

- Talk about how the word *and* is often overused. While it is fine to use it occasionally, written work can be much improved by learning and using a variety of connectives. Write up two facts which can be linked by *and,* e.g.:

    Transport improved in Victorian times. There were many new inventions.

    Demonstrate orally how the sentences can be linked by *and* and by the other devices:

    *Transport improved in Victorian times **and** there were many new inventions.*
    *Transport improved in Victorian times. There were many new inventions **as well**.*
    *Transport improved in Victorian times. There were many new inventions **too**.*
    *Transport improved in Victorian times. **Also** there were many new inventions.*
    *   There were **also** many new inventions.*
    *Transport improved in Victorian times. **Furthermore** there were many new inventions.*
    *Transport improved in Victorian times. **In addition**, there were many new inventions.*
    *Transport improved in Victorian times. **What is more**, there were many new inventions.*

- Ask students in pairs to do the same with another two facts linked by *and*, perhaps related to recent reading or cross-curricular work. The second fact must be purely additional information (young people often use *and* instead of causal or time connectives) so they will have to experiment until they find two facts that work.
- Ask students to feed back their sentences, joined in different ways. Ask which they like the best each time. Perhaps you could take a vote on it.
- On another occasion, use the sentence starts in the box to illustrate how to build an argument without repetition, e.g.:

    *The reason I am in favour of television is that it has many entertainment programmes. **A second reason** is that we can watch important sporting events. Another point is that it keeps everyone up to date with the news. **A further point** is that it is often educational. **Finally**, it lets you watch films in your own home.*

    Help students see that *Also, Furthermore, What is more* and *In addition* could also be substituted here.
- Ask pairs to list arguments for or against something, and then to practise them orally, using a variety of connectives.

These frames can be used when students are expressing their views about fiction or topics across the curriculum.

OPPOSING INFORMATION

but   yet

while   although

whereas

However …

Nevertheless …

On the other hand, …

Despite this …

or …

Alternatively, …

These frames introduce students to alternative ways of saying *but*. A few of these constructions will be familiar from the first *Speaking Frames* book, but this collection is wider and more diverse.

Lesson plan

- Talk about the word *but* and how it introduces an opposite fact or point of view. You could represent this opposition with the symbol >< . In formal writing, *but* should not be used to start a sentence (it is a coordinating conjunction, which technically should always come *between* two chunks of meaning). Students therefore need an alternative to *but* for use in their writing and speech.
  Write up two facts which can be linked by *but,* e.g.:

  I like tomato sauce. I hate tomatoes.

  Ask students to demonstrate orally how these sentences can be linked by *but* and the other devices:

  *I like tomato sauce **but** I hate tomatoes.*
  *I like tomato sauce **yet** I hate tomatoes.*
  *I like tomato sauce **while** I hate tomatoes.*
  *I like tomato sauce **although** I hate tomatoes.*
  *I like tomato sauce **whereas** I hate tomatoes*
  *I like tomato sauce. **However,** I hate tomatoes.*
  *I like tomato sauce. **Nevertheless** I hate tomatoes.*
  *I like tomato sauce. **On the other hand,** I hate tomatoes.*
  *I like tomato sauce **despite the fact that** I hate tomatoes.*

- Ask students in pairs to try linking the following pairs of facts with each of the connectives:

  My friend likes football. I prefer cricket.
  James is a boy. Zoe is a girl.

  As pairs report back, ask the class which versions they do/don't like, and why.
- *But* is a very versatile word and some of the suggested connectives cannot be substituted for all uses of it. Ask students in pairs to search for *but* in texts in the classroom and try substituting the other words – during feedback discuss which ones work in terms of conveying meaning and which don't. You should find that *However* can almost always be substituted.
- On another occasion, look at the use of *but* in providing alternatives. Provide two statements which offer a choice, e.g.:

  James could go to the cinema. He could stay at home.

  and let students link them with ***but, yet, while, However, On the other hand***. This time add in ***or*** and ***Alternatively.*** Discuss which sound the best.
- Ask pairs of students to try the same with other alternative statements:

  It might rain. It might be sunny.
  We can make a sandwich. It might be fun to have a takeaway.

GENERALISATION

probably   possibly

arguably   on the whole

perhaps   maybe

usually   generally   mostly

may   might   could

tend(s)   seem(s)

about   around   circa

approximately   roughly

This frame provides a selection of words and phrases that can be used to introduce generalisations or approximations in descriptive writing. These are important in factual writing to 'cover' the writer when a point is not (or might not be) absolute. They are also used frequently in persuasive writing, where they are sometimes known as 'weasel words' (e.g. '*Probably* the best lager in the world').

Introductory lesson

- Discuss the fact that some 'statements of fact' may be debatable, e.g. *Fish feel no pain when they are caught.* With students try out each of the words above the box (some may be possible in more than one position). Ask students to listen to each construction and decide which they think 'sounds right'.

    > **Probably** *fish feel no pain when they are caught.*
    > *Fish* **probably** *feel no pain when they are caught.*
    > **Possibly** *fish feel no pain* ...   **Arguably** *fish feel no pain* ...
    > **On the whole**, *fish feel no pain* ...   **Perhaps** *fish feel no pain* ...
    > **Maybe** *fish feel no pain* ...   **Usually** *fish feel no pain* ...
    > **Generally** *fish feel no pain* ...   **Mostly**, *fish feel no pain* ...

- You can also make a generalisation by the use of 'tentative' verbs. Ask students to try inserting the verbs in the box, e.g.:

    > *Fish* **may** *feel* ...   *Fish* **might** *feel* ...   *Fish* **could** *feel* ...
    > *Fish* **tend to** *feel* ...   *Fish* **seem to** *feel* ...

- Through discussion, establish that in this case *On the whole, Usually, Generally, Mostly* and *tend to* are inappropriate, as we don't know for sure one way or the other. But they may work for another debatable statement, e.g.:

    > *Boys are better at football than girls.*

    It is as well to have access to a wide range of vocabulary, so you can pick and choose (and vary your expression).

- Ask students in pairs to make up a debatable statement of their own. They should then go through the words, trying each out, and select the three they like best in their sentence.

- Ask a pair of students to feed back their best three sentences. Ask other students to try some of the other contractions and discuss why the pair rejected them. Repeat with a number of pairs, so that the class is exposed to frequent repetition of the 'weasel words'.

- On another occasion look at the words in the bottom box. These words allow you to give an approximation, particularly when you are dealing with numbers, e.g. *The woman was 25 years old: about 25, around 25, approximately 25, roughly 25, circa 25.* Discuss which 'sounds the best' in this and other sentences. Help them recognise that *approximately* is mainly used in scientific writing, and *circa* is often used in history for dates.

> Revisit these frames when students are about to write report, persuasion or discussion texts, to orally rehearse the constructions.

GIVING EXAMPLES

For example, ...   For instance, ...

such as ...   e.g. ...

including ...

like ...

An example of this is ...

An illustration of this is ...

This can be illustrated by ...

Exemplification is required in all types of writing, but particularly in report and persuasive writing. Many students introduce examples with the term *like*, which is frequently inelegant and sometimes grammatically incorrect.

Introductory lesson

● Discuss why it is sometimes necessary to give examples:

   – to back up a point
   – to clarify a description
   – sometimes, instead of a definition or explanation.

● Provide an example, and try it with each, e.g.:

   *There are many breeds of dog. **For example**, there are large dogs like the Great Dane, and small dogs like the Yorkshire Terrier.*
   *There are many breeds of dog. **For instance**, there are large dogs ...*
   *There are many breeds of dog, **e.g.** large dogs ...*
   *There are many breeds of dog, **such as** large dogs ...*
   *There are many breeds of dog, **including** large dogs ...*
   *There are many breeds of dog, **like** large dogs like the Great Dane ...*

   Establish that *like* and *such as* are unsuitable here.
● Establish that certain constructions fit certain situations, e.g.:

   *You should choose a dog to suit your lifestyle. **For example**, city-dwellers should not buy a dog that needs lots of exercise* will work with **For instance** and **e.g.** but none of the others.

● Ask students in pairs to look in non-fiction books to find places where the author has given an example, e.g. our 'Rules for Group Discussion' on page 45 and try substituting the other constructions, to find those that work and those that don't work. Ask pairs to report back, and establish that some constructions work better for lists and others for single specific examples.

> Revisit these frames when students are about to write report, persuasion or discussion texts, to orally rehearse the constructions. Display them as part of the 'writing toolkit' when students are writing.

GIVING DEFINITIONS

_____ , which is ...

_____ . This is ...

_____ (...)

... called _____

... known as _____

_____ who ...

In non-fiction writing, where technical terminology is introduced, writers need access to a variety of ways of embedding definitions in the body of a text.

Introductory lesson

● Discuss how it is often necessary to define the terms you use when writing non-fiction, especially if they are technical terms which the general reader may not know, e.g.:

   *The butterfly feeds through its <u>proboscis</u>, **which** is a tube on the front of its head.*

Explain that in each of our speaking frames, the technical term is represented by a straight line and the definition by a dotted line.

● Write up the example and ask students to try substituting the other constructions:

   *The butterfly feeds through its <u>proboscis</u>. **This** is a tube on the front of its head.*
   *The butterfly feeds through its <u>proboscis</u> **(a tube on the front of its head**).*
   *The butterfly feeds through a tube on the front of its head **called** a <u>proboscis</u>.*
   *The butterfly feeds through a tube on the front of its head **known as** a <u>proboscis</u>.*

● Point out that when you are defining or describing a human being, the introductory word is *who* as opposed to *which*, e.g.:

   *The knight was served by his <u>squire</u>, **who** was usually a young boy training to be a knight.*

Ask students to try substituting all the other constructions.

● Help students recognise that when the definition is plural, *This* has to change to *These*, e.g. *... squires. **These** were usually ...*

● *Ask* students in pairs:

   – either to think up a sentence including a technical term, which they can define
   – or to find an example in non-fiction books, and to try substituting the other constructions. Ask pairs to report back, so that students gain familiarity with all the frames.

Revisit these frames when students are about to write any non-fiction texts in which technical terminology occurs, to orally rehearse the constructions. Display them as part of the 'writing toolkit' when students are writing.

SUMMING UP

On the whole, ...   so I/we conclude ...

Overall, ...   I/we therefore conclude ...

In conclusion, ...

This leads me/us to conclude ...

Taking everything into account ...

After due consideration ...

believe   think

feel   agree

This selection of words and phrases can be used at the end of a persuasion or discussion text, when the author presents his/her final conclusions.

Introductory lesson

- Discuss the meaning of *conclusion* in the context of persuasion and discussion text (i.e. deciding on a point of view after weighing all the evidence/arguments). Give an example, e.g. **On the whole**, *the arguments in favour of homework seem to outweigh those against,* **so** *I do not think it should be banned.*
- Explain that the two sets of frames are interchangeable, as are the four alternatives to the verb *conclude* in the box on the right. Write up your example and ask students to try substituting the other frames, to see how many different ways they can express a final conclusion. Have some pairs feed back to the class so they all become familiar with the constructions.
- Ask students in pairs to:

  - imagine another debatable topic, e.g. *foxhunting*
  - decide on whether the arguments **for** or **against** would win
  - fill in the frames appropriately
  - try as many substitutions as they can.

  Ask some pairs to feed back some of their completed frames to the class.

Revisit these frames when students are about to write persuasion or discussion texts, to orally rehearse the constructions. Display them as part of the 'writing toolkit' when students are writing.

EVIDENCE FROM THE TEXT

This is illustrated on page _____ where _____
_____ .

We know this because on page _____ the author says
_____ .

The evidence for this is on page _____ where _____
_____ .

The words that tell us this are _____ on page _____
_____ .

On page _____ , the author says _____ .

This suggests that _____ .

indicates implies shows

Simpler versions of some of these frames appear in the first *Speaking Frames* book. They introduce the importance of evidence, especially in reading, to help students justify their inferences. Critical reading – 'interrogating the text' – is a good preparation for critical thinking in general and thus intellectual good health. All students are capable of critical thought, but articulating reasons for opinions and impressions is not easy, so the more help we can give the better.

Introductory lesson

- Introduce the term *evidence* (proof) and talk about why it is important to provide evidence for our impressions.
- Use an example of inference from your current reading, and provide the evidence. Ask students to use each of the speaking frames to express it. Explain that the verbs in the box at the bottom of the page may be substituted for *suggests* in the final frame, depending on which seems most appropriate for the particular point. All these words are useful for students to have in their repertoire when providing evidence, so it's worth giving many opportunities for practice. (Note: another word frequently used in this context is *infers*. Technically, this actually means 'draws the conclusion', so it is the reader who infers something from the text. This meaning is gradually changing because of usage, but at present it's probably still worth discouraging students from using it.)
- Set another question relating to current reading (or a number of questions for different groups) and ask students to discuss in pairs, find the evidence and express it using each of the frames. In feedback, ensure they hear each of the frames several times.

> This set of frames can be used frequently during reading to help students formulate and articulate the reasons behind their responses to text.

OPPOSING VIEWPOINTS

On the one hand   On the other (hand)

Some people ...   Others/other people

Supporters of ...   Opponents (of ...)

Those in favour of ...   Those against ...

People who approve of ... Critics ...

say   claim   believe

maintain   argue   contend

reply   respond

This page collects together some key vocabulary and sentence frames for dealing with the explanation of two sides of a question.

Introductory lesson

- Point out that when you are explaining an argument, phrases like *On the one hand ..., on the other hand* act as important signals to your audience that you are moving from one side of the argument to the other. There is more useful vocabulary for signalling you are moving to an opposing view on page 70 in *Opposing information.*
- You also have to give the participants in the argument names of some sort. For instance, in an argument about the pros and cons of smoking, you could refer to *smokers* and *non-smokers.* Usually, however, there are no such convenient labels and you need a range of ways of referring to the two sides.
- Another important element in explaining an argument is the use of a range of verbs to substitute for the obvious verb 'say', which would be most students' choice in spontaneous speech. The verbs in the box can be used with any of the frames.
- Illustrate the use of the discussion frames (including the selection of verbs) with an example, e.g. pros and cons of homework:

  Some people maintain that homework is useful because ... Others claim that ...

- Ask students to do the same with the remaining frames, e.g.:

  Supporters of homework contend that ... Opponents of homework reply that ...
  Those in favour of homework argue that ... Those against respond that ...
  People who support homework believe ... Critics say ...

When students are familiar with the frames, they can be used during any discussion or debate in any curriculum area.

Appendix: Learning, language and literacy across the curriculum

The following edited extracts from *How to Teach Writing Across the Curriculum: Ages 8–14* explain the 'two horses' model of teaching more fully, showing how speaking frames fit into the overall framework. For more detail, case studies and teaching materials, *How to Teach Writing Across the Curriculum: Ages 8–14*.

The two horses model for cross-curricular literacy

You can't teach children to write before they can talk. It's putting the cart before the horse.

It's over a decade now since a teacher in Yorkshire uttered those words at one of my inservice courses. As I drove home that night I started wondering exactly how teachers could ensure that the 'horse' of talk was properly hitched up to draw the 'cart' of writing.

Eventually, after long conversations with many colleagues I concluded that, in order to write, students need two sorts of talk:

- talk for learning – plenty of opportunities to use the simple spontaneous language of speech to ensure they understand the ideas and content they're going to write about;
- talk for writing – opportunities to meet and internalise the relevant patterns of 'literate language', to help them turn that content into well crafted sentences.

So students need not one but two 'horses' to draw the writing 'cart':

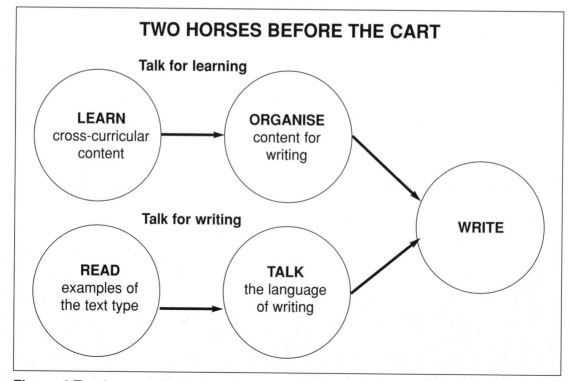

TWO HORSES BEFORE THE CART

Talk for learning

LEARN
cross-curricular
content

ORGANISE
content for
writing

Talk for writing

READ
examples of
the text type

TALK
the language
of writing

WRITE

Figure 4 Two horses before the cart basic model

Talk for learning

Learn cross-curricular content

In order to understand the content of cross-curricular teaching, apprentice writers need – just as they have always needed – plenty of opportunities for talk. These are provided through the sort of 'active learning' that provides opportunities for speaking and listening, such as:

- opportunities for imaginative engagement – drama, role-play, 'hot-seating';
- outings, excursions, field trips and other opportunities to find out about the wider world through experience and talk to a range of adults;
- active engagement in learning whenever possible: experimenting, making pictures, models, collages, websites, 'TV documentaries' etc (there are now so many ways of creating audio and video records of learning activities);
- audio-visual aids for learning – for instance, relevant items to look at, touch and talk about;
- storytelling – listening to adults telling stories and anecdotes, and having opportunities to tell them themselves;
- responding to ideas through music, movement, art and craft.

Of course, in addition, students need opportunities to talk about and around ideas, through frequent opportunities for paired talk, and group or class discussion.

Such opportunities for active, motivating learning should be provided in all areas of the curriculum, whether by subject specialists in secondary school or by the class teacher in top primary. With so much attention these days to 'pencil and paper' work, it is sometimes tempting to think that they're a waste of valuable time. In fact, they're essential not only for learning, but for language and literacy development – and they're the obvious way to make the best use of cross-curricular links to literacy.

Experience has shown that certain types of active learning sit particularly comfortably with the different text types we use for cross-curricular writing, as shown in the boxes below. These activities reflect the underlying structures of thought upon which the text types depend, and thus link to the planning skeletons described in the next section.

Organise content for learning

The different text types are characterised by their underlying structures – the ways that particular types of information are organised for writing. Awareness of these structures can become a powerful aid to understanding, allowing students to organise their learning in the form of notes or pictures before – or **instead of** – writing.

Skeletons for writing

I originally devised the 'skeleton' frameworks shown in the box for the English National Literacy Strategy. At the time, we called them 'graphic organisers' or 'diagrammatic representations', neither of which was a snappy title to use with primary children. It was a boy in the north east of England who christened them. He rushed up to his teacher with the words: 'They're skeletons, aren't they, Miss? They're the skeletons that you hang the writing on!' Thanks to that unknown Geordie lad, the skeleton frameworks became instantly memorable.

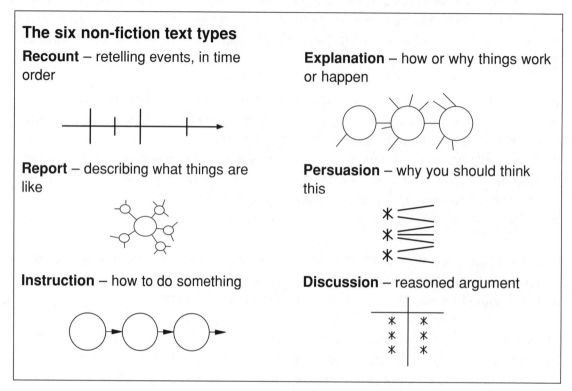

The six non-fiction text types

Recount – retelling events, in time order

Explanation – how or why things work or happen

Report – describing what things are like

Persuasion – why you should think this

Instruction – how to do something

Discussion – reasoned argument

Figure 5 A range of skeletons

How to use skeletons

Skeleton planning provides a link between cross-curricular content and specific teaching of writing skills. All teachers (whether or not they're responsible for literacy teaching) can introduce students to these ways of organising ideas by:

● demonstrating how to use skeletons themselves as simple note-taking devices and aide memoires throughout the curriculum;
● teaching students how to draw the skeletons, and recognise which sorts of ideas and texts are associated with each skeleton;
● sending skeleton notes to the literacy lesson, so they can be used to link knowledge and understanding acquired in a wide range of subject areas with the literacy skills required to record that understanding.

Debbie Billard, a teacher in Rotherham, coined the term 'memory-joggers' for the jottings on a skeleton framework. She explains that memory-joggers are not proper sentences, nor do they have to be words at all. Notes, diagrams, symbols, pictures, photographs are all acceptable – anything that will jog the memory when one comes to write.

The skeleton can then be used like a carrier bag to bring this cross-curricular content to the literacy or English lesson. Once students have been taught the relevant language features of recount text, they can use their memory-joggers to write. Debbie's suggestion is to 'turn your memory-joggers into sentences'.

Teachers who have used skeleton frameworks with their classes have pointed out a number of advantages:

- making skeleton notes helps students organise what they have learned to aid memorisation of the facts;
- many students (especially boys) find it helpful to make this kind of 'big picture' record, so they have an overview of the whole piece of writing before beginning to write (which is, by its nature, a linear sequential process, rather than a holistic one);
- today's students are highly visually literate and skeleton planning helps them use visual memory skills to aid learning;
- as students learn a repertoire of skeletons, they can use them to take notes for a variety of purposes, not just as a precursor to writing;
- skeletons allow teachers and students to make clear links between literacy skills and the rest of the curriculum;
- planning on a skeleton allows students to organise the content of their writing in advance (including dividing material into sections and paragraphing) – it means that when they actually settle down to write, they can concentrate entirely on the language of writing;
- making a skeleton with the class provides an opportunity for highly focused speaking and listening;
- making a skeleton with a partner is an excellent focus for paired talk;
- using skeletons develops students' thinking skills.

It seems clear from talking to teachers that skeletons have the potential to be more than simple planning devices for writing. Perhaps the most exciting suggestion is that skeleton planning can become a way of developing generic thinking skills – helping students recognise the different ways human beings organise their ideas, depending on the subject matter we're addressing.

Talk for writing

Once students securely understand the content they are to write about, they need help in acquiring appropriate language structures to express it. Each of the text types is characterised by certain language features. The teaching of cross-curricular writing therefore provides many opportunities for revisiting aspects of grammar within a purposeful writing context.

However, care should always be taken not to *over-focus* on grammatical or stylistic elements at the expense of meaning. This is why 'word' and 'sentence' level teaching are best covered separately from meaningful writing tasks. 'Shared Writing' then provides an opportunity to illustrate how these elements are used in writing, referring to them briefly and tangentially without interfering with the overall flow.

It's also important that students' own assessment of their work should not be a mere exercise in box-ticking against a checklist of language features. When teaching focuses on the bureaucracy of learning at the expense of the meaningful whole, there's a price to pay in students' motivation, understanding and – in the long run – ability to write (and think) well and fluently.

Read examples of text type

Reading, in any aspect of literacy, should always precede writing. Every teacher knows that students who read lots of fiction for pleasure tend also to be good at writing fiction – they absorb the rhythms and patterns of narrative language through repeated exposure. They also pick up new vocabulary by meeting it in context. Nowadays however, with the ready availability of screen based entertainment, fewer students see the point of reading for pleasure, so fewer of them tend to be 'natural' storytellers.

This has, in fact, always been the case with non-fiction writing. The non-fiction text types described in the previous section have various textual characteristics with which writers need to be familiar, but only the most voracious readers of non-fiction are likely to be familiar with them (and then, usually, only in limited genres).

Reading aloud

The most obvious way to expose all students to literate language patterns is to read well written non-fiction aloud – magazine and blog articles, short sections from text books, and so on. This helps familiarise them – via their ears – with the vocabulary and language patterns of the text types. As Robert Louis Stevenson put it, this is an excellent way of sensitising young minds to *'the chime of fine words and the march of the stately period'*.

Another excellent strategy is to provide opportunities for students to read non-fiction texts aloud themselves. This gives them the chance to hear literate language patterns produced from their own mouths; to know how standard English and sophisticated vocabulary *feels*; to respond physically to the ebb and flow of well-constructed sentences, learning incidentally how punctuation guides meaning and expression. There's a pay off in both speech and writing when we let accomplished authors put words into our students' mouths.

Reading aloud has acquired a bad reputation in recent years. The traditional technique of 'reading round the class' is embarrassing for poor readers and excruciatingly boring for good ones. But there are other ways of giving students opportunities to read decent texts aloud.

One is **paired reading**, when two students share a book or short text, dividing the reading between them. Depending on their level of ability, this could be alternate pages or alternate paragraphs. (For special needs students, reading alternate sentences encourages them to look for the full stops, and thus take note of sentence boundaries.)

When the class needs some subject knowledge, paired reading of a text is a good way to provide it.

Another is **reader's theatre**, when a group of students are asked to prepare an oral presentation of a short text for the rest of the class. There's no room here to describe it at length, but you'll find plenty of details and good ideas on the internet.

Talk the language of writing

Speaking frames

We can also provide opportunities for students to innovate on written language patterns by creating speaking frames for the sorts of vocabulary and sentence structures we want them to produce in their writing.

Our 'two horses' model for cross-curricular writing now looks like this:

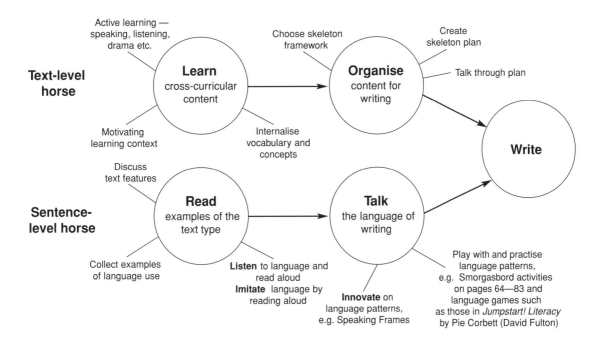

Figure 6 Two horses before the cart model

However, while the structured 'talk for writing' exercises in this *Speaking Frames* book are designed to familiarize students with literate language patterns, they also need frequent opportunities to put these to use across the curriculum. 'Talk for learning' and 'talk for writing' should be regularly combined in formal speaking activities, such as:

- debates and panel discussions, e.g. 'Question Time';
- commentary and voice-overs on students' own audio or TV productions;
- individual short talks or interviews on aspects of cross-curricular work;
- group presentations to other classes or outside audiences;
- role-play activities (e.g. TV interviews, political speeches) in which students argue a case in the role of the expert.

Supporting writing across the curriculum in secondary schools

How to Teach Writing Across the Curriculum: Ages 8–14 (Routledge) shows how to make links between learning across the curriculum and the teaching of literacy. Since English teachers have major responsibility for literacy development, the book is primarily aimed at them. But subject specialists are also responsible for developing 'key skills' relevant to their fields of study – so they too need to be aware of significant aspects of non-fiction writing. The relevant elements are described in detail in *How to Teach Writing Across the Curriculum*, especially the skeleton system of recording understanding (see the two photocopiable handouts at the end of this book).

Broadly speaking, if subject specialists cover the 'top horse' in the 'two horses' model (talk for learning), English teachers can use students' cross-curricular learning to develop the 'bottom horse' (talk for writing), and show how to convert that learning into written language. If English teachers can convince colleagues of the value of following the model, there are clear advantages for all teachers and students – not least in terms of time spent on recording students' learning:

- non-English specialists are relieved of the responsibility of *teaching* writing skills, allowing them to concentrate on their own subject area;
- English specialists have ready-made meaningful content for literacy lessons, which they can use to develop students' speaking and writing skills.

Since effort is no longer being duplicated (possibly at cross-purposes) it should also free up time for all teachers to provide more opportunities for 'active learning', especially for developing ideas and understanding through talk. The following three handouts cover the information about cross-curricular writing non-English specialists need to know.

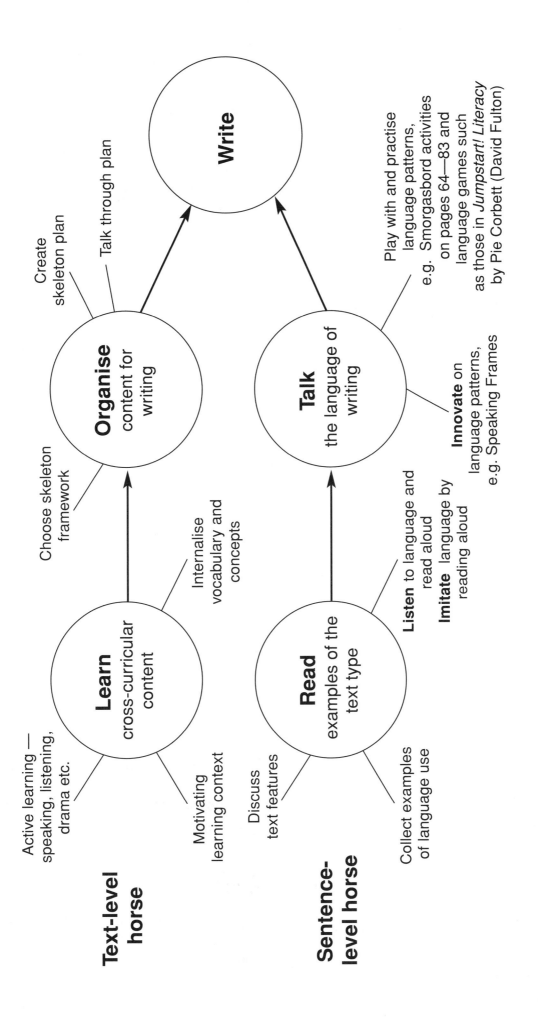

Text-level horse

Learn cross-curricular content
- Active learning — speaking, listening, drama etc.
- Motivating learning context
- Internalise vocabulary and concepts

Organise content for writing
- Choose skeleton framework
- Create skeleton plan
- Talk through plan

Write

Sentence-level horse

Read examples of the text type
- Discuss text features
- Collect examples of language use
- **Listen** to language and read aloud
- **Imitate** language by reading aloud

Talk the language of writing
- **Innovate** on language patterns, e.g. Speaking Frames
- Play with and practise language patterns, e.g. Smorgasbord activities on pages 64—83 and language games such as those in *Jumpstart! Literacy* by Pie Corbett (David Fulton)

The six non-fiction text types
and their application across the curriculum

Recount

retelling events in time order

accounts of schoolwork/outings
stories from history or RE
anecdotes and personal accounts
biographical writing in any subject

Report

describing what something is (or was) like

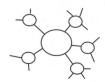

aspects of life in a historical period
characteristics of plants/animals
descriptions of localities/geographical features

Explanation

explaining how/why something happens

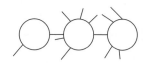

why historical events happened
how things work/come about in science,
    geography, etc.

Instruction

telling how to do or make something

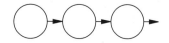

art, DT, PE activities
procedures in maths/ICT/science
class or school rules

Persuasion

arguing a case; trying to influence opinion

'publicity campaigns' (articles, posters, leaflets)
    in any subject
expressing viewpoints on controversial topics in
    any subject

Discussion

a balanced argument

stating the case on both sides of a controversy
    in any subject
writing objective 'essays'

The key ingredients of non-fiction text types

Recount	Report	Explanation	Instruction	Persuasion	Discussion

Audience Someone who is interested in what happened	**Audience** Someone who wants to know about something	**Audience** Someone who wants to understand a process	**Audience** Someone who wants to know how to do something	**Audience** Someone you are trying to influence	**Audience** Someone who is interested in an issue
Purpose To tell the reader what happened in an informative and entertaining way	**Purpose** To present information so that it is easy to find and understand	**Purpose** To help someone understand a process	**Purpose** To tell someone how to do something clearly	**Purpose** To promote a particular view in order to influence what people do or think	**Purpose** To help someone understand the issue
Examples • autobiography • newspaper article • history book	**Examples** • dictionary • reference book • text books	**Examples** • car manual • encyclopaedia • science text book	**Examples** • recipe • instruction manual	**Examples** • adverts • fliers • newspaper editorial	**Examples** • news feature • essay on causes of something e.g. global warming
Typical structure • paragraphs organised in chronological order	**Typical structure** • paragraphs – not in chronological order • often organised in categories with headings/sub-headings	**Typical structure** • series of logical steps explaining how or why something occurs	**Typical structure** • chronological order • often in list form • diagrams, visual	**Typical structure** • often a series of points supporting one viewpoint • logical order	**Typical structure** • paragraphs • often a series of contrasting points • logical order
Typical language features • past tense • first or third person • time connectives	**Typical language features** • formal and impersonal • technical vocabulary • present tense • generalises • detail where necessary	**Typical language features** • casual connectives • technical vocabulary • formal and impersonal • present tense	**Typical language features** • simple and clear formal English • imperative • numbers or time connectives	**Typical language features** • emotive language • personal language • weasel phrases	**Typical language features** • present tense • formal and impersonal • logical connectives

With thanks to Julia Strong of the National Literacy Trust

David Fulton Books

Second Editions

How to Teach Writing Across the Curriculum

Sue Palmer   *Series: Writers' Workshop*

Now in updated second editions, *How to Teach Writing Across the Curriculum: Ages 6–8* and *8–14* provides a range of practical suggestions for teaching non-fiction writing skills and linking them to children's learning across the curriculum. With new hints and tips for teachers and suggestions for reflective practice, these books will equip teachers with all the skills and materials needed to create enthusiastic non-fiction writers in their classroom.

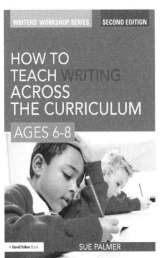

Ages 6–8
August 2010: A4: 112pp
Pb: 978-0-415-57990-2:
£19.99

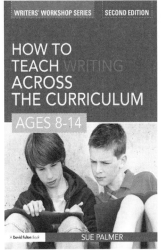

Ages 8–14
August 2010: A4: 112pp
Pb: 978-0-415-57991-9:
£19.99

Includes:

- techniques for using speaking and listening, drama and games to prepare for writing
- suggestions for the use of cross-curricular learning as a basis for writing
- planning frameworks and 'skeletons' for children to use
- information on key language features of non-fiction texts
- examples of non-fiction writing
- guidance on the process of creating writing from note-making.

New Material: More emphasis on creativity and the creative process – giving teachers more suggestions for working with the freed up curriculum. New pedagogical features with teacher 'hints and tips' have been added throughout.

Includes:

- information on the organisation and language features of the six main non-fiction text types
- suggestions for the use of cross-curricular learning as a basis for writing
- planning frameworks for children to use
- advice on developing children's writing to help with organisational issues
- examples of non-fiction writing
- suggestions for talk for learning and talk for writing
- information on the transition from primary to secondary school.

New Material: The two horses teaching model is introduced with extended material on speaking and listening. There is additional material on transitions and the early secondary level and photocopiable resources for teachers and recommended resources have been updated.

 **Routledge** Taylor & Francis Group   **www.routledge.com/teachers**